CALLing All Foreign Language Teachers

Computer-Assisted Language Learning in the Classroom

Edited by

Tony Erben & Iona Sarieva

EYE ON EDUCATION

EYE ON EDUCATION

6 DEPOT WAY WEST, SUITE 106

LARCHMONT, NY 10538

(914) 833–0551

(914) 833–0761 fax

www.eyeoneducation.com

For information about permission to reproduce selections from this book, write: Eye On Education, Permissions Dept., Suite 106, 6 Depot Way West, Larchmont, NY 10538.

Library of Congress Cataloging-in-Publication Data

Erben, Tony.

CALLing all foreign language teachers : computer-assisted language learning in the classroom / Tony Erben.

p. cm.

ISBN 978-1-59667-069-3

1. Language and languages—Study and teaching—Technological innovations. I. Title.

P53.855.E73 2007

418.0078—dc22

10 9 8 7 6 5 4 3 2 1   2007032306

Also Available from EYE ON EDUCATION

Differentiated Instruction:
A Guide for Foreign Language Teachers
Deborah Blaz

Bringing the Standards for
Foreign Language Learning to Life
Deborah Blaz

Activities, Games, and Assessment Strategies,
for the Foreign Language Classroom
Amy Buttner

100 Games and Activities for the
Introductory Foreign Language Classroom
Thierry Boucquey, et al.

A Collection of Performance Tasks
and Rubrics: Foreign Languages
Deborah Blaz

Foreign Language Teacher's Guide to Active Learning
Deborah Blaz

Teaching Foreign Languages in the Block
Deborah Blaz

What Great Teachers Do Differently:
14 Things That Matter Most
Todd Whitaker

Seven Simple Secrets:
What the Best Teachers Know and Do!
Annette Breaux and Todd Whitaker

Classroom Motivation from A to Z:
How to Engage Your Students in Learning
Barbara R. Blackburn

Meet the Contributors

James Aubry has taught French for many years at the University of South Florida and is currently a Visiting Assistant Professor of French at the University of Tampa.

Sha Balize, Ph.D., specializes in assessment & evaluation in foreign language and ESOL. She currently works for Education Testing Services in Austin, Texas.

Ruth Ban, Ph.D., has been a teacher of Spanish and ESOL. She has lived and taught baccalaureate courses in Mexico for over 20 years and is currently an Assistant Professor of ESOL at Barry University, Florida.

Martha Castañeda, Ph.D., is an Assistant Professor of Foreign language Education / ESOL at the University of Miami in Ohio. She specializes in the application of technology in Spanish classes.

Zhaohui Chen, Ph.D., graduated form the Second Language Acquisition / Instructional technology program at the University of South Florida. He is currently working for a company in Oregon that specializes in the creation of online standardized ESOL and foreign language tests for educational organizations across the country. His language specialization is Chinese.

Rui Cheng, Ph.D., is a program specialist for Blackboard course management software and faculty development with regards to technology at the Sarasota campus of the University of South Florida. Her language specialization is Chinese.

Deborah Cordier is currently and Instructor of French and a student in the Second Language Acquisition / Instructional technology program at the University of South Florida.

Kristina Eisenhower, formerly a student in the Second Language Acquisition/Instructional technology program at the University of South Florida.

Tony Erben, Ph.D., formerly Associate Professor of FLE/ESOL and Co-coordinator of the FLE/ESOL program at USF, now, Director of the ESOL Program at the University of Tampa. He has published widely is the area of technology use in FLE and ESOL. His languages include German and Japanese.

Aline Harrison is an ESOL/Spanish content specialist who has worked for the past decade with the Belize Ministry of Education. She is currently finishing her Ph.D. in Higher Education at USF.

Jane Harvey is currently a student in the Second Language Acquisition / Instructional technology program at the University of South Florida. She has had wide teaching experiences in Turkey, England and Italy. Her languages include French and Turkish.

Li Jin, Ph.D., is currently an Assistant Professor of Chinese at Appalachian University in North Carolina. She has published widely in the area of technology use in foreign language classrooms.

Ray Madrigal, Ph.D., is currently an Assistant Professor of Spanish and Classical Languages at Florida Southern College in Tampa.

Ruth Roux-Rodriguez, Ph.D., has for many years taught Spanish and English in Mexico at the University level.

Iona Sarieva is currently a student in the Second Language Acquisition / Instructional technology program at the University of South Florida. She is trilingual in Russian, Bulgarian and English.

Sabine Siekman, Ph.D., is an Assistant Professor of Applied Linguistics at the University of Alaska in Fairbanks. She is an expert in distance learning and has many years of experience in teaching German as a foreign language.

Robert Summers is Director of the Language Laboratory at State University of New York at Albany. He has many years of experience in teaching French through technology.

Annmarie Zoran, Ph.D., is an ESOL instructor in Slovenia. She has published widely in the area of technology use in ESOL and FLE.

Table of Contents

1

Introduction: CALLing All Foreign Language Teachers

Tony Erben

Hello fellow foreign language teachers!

This book is the result of four years of effort. It sprang out of a desire to provide foreign language teachers with a comprehensive guide and framework for using and integrating technology into their classrooms.

For the past 20 years, I have been teaching technology classes to pre-service and in-service foreign language and English as a second language teachers, and I have noticed over the years that there is a lack of materials for teachers that provide a guide to learn how to use an array of technologies and once learned, a systematic way to infuse technology into the teaching and learning practices of both teachers and learners. I hope that we can fill the gap with this volume.

For ease of use, *CALLing All Foreign Language Teachers* is divided into 6 sections and 18 chapters. We are particularly excited about the many practical, student-centered activities highlighted throughout Chapters 4 through 17. Each activity is framed within the American Council for the Teaching of Foreign Languages (ACTFL) standards as well as ISTE's (International Society for Technology in Education) National Educational Technology Standards (NETS). Section I, "Incorporating Computer-Assisted Language Learning," provides readers with the principles that frame this book and summarizes the research on which the work in each chapter is based. For example, in Chapter 2, Iona Sarieva and Annmarie Zoran use an easy-to-read question-and-answer format to outline how the discipline of second language acquisition and computer-mediated language learning supplies handy signposts for research-based teaching practices using technology in second and foreign language environments. Elucidating the need for an informed application of technology in the classroom, Sarieva and Zoran point to work that is being carried out in the field of instructional technology that can help foreign language teachers make their technology-infused pedagogical practices more constructivist in intent and scope.

In Chapter 3, "Using Technology for Foreign Language Instruction: Creative Innovations, Research, and Applications," Tony Erben, Ruth Ban, Li Jin, Robert Summers, and Kristina Eisenhower provide a lucid overview of the outcomes of research on the use of technology in foreign and second language learning environments. Their analysis of this research provides the reader with a handy, research-based list of do's and don'ts for teachers who are using technology, as well as a description of the types of students we can expect to have in our classroom. These students belong to the "digital generation," for whom computers, iPods, cell phones, the Web, chat rooms, and instant messaging are the norm. In the case of technology, it is often the intermediate school student who can teach us a thing or two about technology. However, this book tries to right the imbalance! We are still trained foreign language teachers with the methodological and pedagogical know-how to teach a foreign language. With this book, foreign language teachers can get their heads around the technology. Ultimately, the marriage of technology and foreign language can help us, as a profession, to rethink, reshape, and reinvent the nature of curriculum engagement, delivery, and learning processes to reflect something that is closer to 21st-century notions of education. Finally, Erben and colleagues provide a sneak preview of what is around the corner in terms of new technologies and their impact on teaching.

Chapter 4 introduces, or better still, re-introduces teachers to a number of well used technologies. We thought it would be sensible to start teachers off on technologies they know before introducing a world of technologies they don't know. So, for starters Aubry, Balize, Chen, Siekman, Sarieva, and Roux-Rodriguez have put together a compilation of unique activities centered around word processing, email, and building websites.

Section II, "E-Creation," is all about using software tools to create resources that will support your teaching and the learning of your students. Sabine Siekmann, Iona Sarieva, and Ruth Roux-Rodriguez show the many ways in which word processing can be used other than for document writing. In Chapter 5, Robert Summers and Ray Madrigal present a much sought-after explanation of the ways in which Microsoft PowerPoint can be used in foreign language classrooms other than for presentation purposes. They outline PowerPoint's capabilities for creating interactive games that promote second language interaction among students and increase motivation. Another software package that enables both teachers and students to create cards, posters, and other materials that incorporate visuals is Microsoft Publisher. Here, Martha Castañeda and Rui Cheng take readers through the process of creating a cornucopia of visually exciting curriculum materials. In keeping with the theme of creating visually exciting materials. Sabine Siekmann shows readers, in Chapter 7, how to create sound files and import them into Web pages, as well as how to use sound files for teaching and learning purposes. Finally, Rui Cheng and Robert Summers explain how to create and edit online movies using both Mac and PC computers. Their chapter is timely, as it presents software that readily brings together oral, aural, visual, and written media in one online package.

As the name suggests, the section on "E-Communication" centers on software packages that allow teachers and students to engage in various forms of interaction. In Chapter 9, Rui Cheng and Martha Castañeda outline the benefits of joining Listservs. Of course, there are thousands of Listservs on the Internet, but for foreign language teachers and learners, there are specific Listservs that empower both teachers and students by bringing them together as part of a much wider world community of learners. In the next chapter, Sha Balizet presents the reader with ways that teachers can access and use synchronous and asynchronous communication systems through chat and e-mail. Finally, Zhaohui Chen and Debra Cordier introduces a new communication system called Skype, which allows learners to use their computer as a telephone and communicate with anybody in the world. It allows not only real-time speaking but also two-way video and voice recording. More importantly, Chen and Cordier shows us how this newest technology can be used in the foreign language classroom in a variety of innovative and exciting ways.

The next section comprises three chapters and in their own way, they are very important. Under "E-Extensions," Iona Sarieva and Annmarie Zoran introduce Nicenet, a free course-management system similar to Blackboard and WebCT. Aline Harrison's outline on WebQuests in Chapter 13, introduces us to inquiry-based tasks in which the user is guided to scan specific Web sites to accomplish a certain task. Harrison provides useful links to Web sites where foreign language teachers have developed WebQuests. In Chapter 14, "Exercise Builder: Using Hot Potatoes," Zhaohui Chen presents us with an online tool that enables teachers to create a variety of activities.

The penultimate section takes us to that part of the curriculum that no teacher or student can do without: assessment. In this section, Rui Cheng in "Electronic Portfolios" and Ruth Ban and Jane Harvey in "Electronic Surveys: Inquiring With Authentic Language," discuss alternative assessment strategies that can improve the ways in which teachers evaluate student performances. Cheng shows the reader how to create and use electronic portfolios using the Microsoft Excel. She talks about the practicalities of using online portfolios to showcase students' work. Complementing Cheng's chapter, Ban and Harvey describe SurveyMonkey and other online survey tools and explain how to use these as pedagogical tools in the classroom.

Last, but not least of all, the final section encourages readers to embark on their own ongoing journey with technology in their own foreign language classrooms. Unlike our students, we foreign language teachers do not belong to the digital generation; however, we can more aptly relate to our students through the use of technology in our teaching. In Chapter 17, Erben provides readers with an array of ready-made technology-infused activities. Each activity accesses multiple technologies and integrates all of the previously presented technologies. The last chapter by Annmarie Zoran encapsulates what the Internet stands for—namely, a world wide forum of information. Some of it is extraordinarily good and useful, and some of it is just plain bad. The task before us is to sift through the good, the bad, and the ugly and to access Web sites that are student and teacher friendly, particularly those that are user friendly to the foreign language learner. In "Gates in Cyberland," Zoran has collated a wonderful array of Web sites for foreign language teachers, as well as language-specific sites and teacher-oriented and learner-oriented sites.

Finally, I want to thank each and every contributor to this book. First, I wish to thank Iona Sarieva, my coeditor, whose help, dogged tenacity, and attention to detail helped to make this book a reality. Second, I want to thank all of the authors, most of whom are practicing foreign language instructors yet, at the time this book was written, had another life as students in the doctoral program in second language acquisition and instructional technology at the University of South Florida. All of them participated in a course called "Applications of Technology to SLA/FLE," and this volume is the result of their labors. Now, many have graduated and started their own academic careers at other institutions of higher learning, both in the United States and overseas.

Dear reader, it is our collective hope that once you have read through this book and tried out the many technologies and activities described here, you will continue to embrace new technologies as they are invented. Indeed, we can already see a half dozen new software products that will continue to transform the work that we will do in the coming years—their names will undoubtedly become a part of the English language, just as they will become a part of our learning lives. These include wikis, blogs, podcasts, interactive television, and iPods, to name but a few. Stay tuned, but for now, please enjoy *CALLing All Foreign Language Teachers*.

These up and coming technologies will be featured, with accompanying activities, on a website at the University of Tampa. The aim of this website will be to keep updating the materials in this book with fresh ideas and activities using the latest technologies as they develop and are invented. You will find these online pages at: http://utweb.ut.edu/Faculty/terben/ CALL.html. Your password is CALL7069-3.

Section I

Incorporating Computer-Assisted Language Learning

2

Guiding Principles: Second Language Acquisition, Instructional Technology, and the Constructivist Framework

Iona Sarieva and Annmarie Zoran

What Standards?

During the late 1990s, the American Council on the Teaching of Foreign Languages, working together with a task group, designed content standards known as the "5 Cs" to be applied in the K–12 curriculum (ACTFL, 1996). The 5 Cs—communications, cultures, connections, comparisons, and communities—were designed to improve foreign language education. Schools have turned to these standards as a framework for the development of materials and curricula for foreign language programs. One of the goals of this book is to incorporate the 5 Cs in a technology-enhanced environment for foreign language learning to achieve the common goal of developing and maintaining proficiency in at least one foreign language (ACTFL, 1996).

In addition, standards have also been developed by the International Society for Technology in Education for both students (NET*S; see ISTE, 2000) and teachers (NET*T; see ISTE, 2000); the goal of these standards is to create a mechanism for the smooth and seamless integration of technology into the curriculum, thereby empowering teachers to use technology in their classrooms to develop higher-order thinking skills and to participate in other discourse communities. We have used both the ACTFL and ISTE standards as the basis of the materials developed for this book in order to facilitate knowledge construction and language learning within our nation's schools.

What Is Technology Integration?

Integrating technology for the mere purpose of using technology should not be the goal of any foreign language program. However, integrating technology can empower foreign language teachers to enhance language learning and provide a platform for achieving standards.

Jolene Dockstader (1999) makes a distinction between what technology integration is and is not: Technology integration should not be considered a "cybersitter" for students, nor should it be used without a purpose. Technology integration, according to Dockstader, should be used to "enhance student learning," to have "curriculum driven technology usage," and to organize "the goals of curriculum and technology into a coordinated, harmonious whole." Technology has many purposes: It can be used to provide more in-depth information on a specific topic, to access authentic target language materials, to gain experience with electronic literacy, or to provide opportunities for interaction with native speakers or other learners of the target language (Warschauer, 1999). Classroom technology use facilitates higher thinking skills and knowledge construction and helps students learn to find, analyze, and synthesize information.

Is Mediated Learning for Me?

Have you used group work in your classroom? Do you believe that collaborative work increases learning? Do you communicate your ideas through different media, such as e-mail and paper notes, or just orally? Do you use authentic material to bring the foreign language into the classroom? If you answered yes, then mediated learning is for you! The concept of mediated learning and the constructivist approach look at learning as blocks that build on what we already know, as opposed to the behaviorist approach, which views learning as a tabula rasa (Kanuka & Anderson, 1999). Mediated learning builds knowledge using a variety of tools to achieve this goal efficiently and effectively as an ongoing and active process of learning. Within mediated learning, the teacher is viewed as a facilitator of knowledge, guiding learners through a process of learning (Lantolf & Appel, 1994; Vygotsky, 1978). Students are encouraged to be active learners who become involved in their own learning process by engaging with one another, with the teacher, and with the material presented to them. Guiding the learner through active engagement and interaction increases the possibilities for learning. As facilitators, we have many tools at our disposal to mediate this type of active learning and to make it a more meaningful and authentic experience. The tools described throughout this book are intended as a springboard for real-world ideas and activities that foreign language educators can use in their classrooms and can share with their students, peers, and community (Alavi & Leidner, 2001).

Changing Instructional Strategies?

We know that many of us teach the way we were taught. Previously, educators could afford to move at a slower pace and reiterate old strategies that were tried and true. Nowadays, the accumulation of information is tremendously fast, and as educators, we have an obligation to keep up with this speedy accumulation of technological and knowledge capital in order to meet the expectations that society places on our students and on us as teachers. Technology, and the access that it gives us to the World Wide Web, empowers teachers with a vast amount of information and flexible tools that provide opportunities to progress from being simply a source of knowledge to becoming a facilitator who takes learners to the proverbial fountain of knowledge and motivates them to drink from it. Technology provides teachers with opportunities to create a rich language environment, to increase interaction, to focus on meaning, and to amplify the positive impact of education on students (Chapelle, 2001). Furthermore, new technology is not simply a teaching tool—it is becoming an essential medium for literacy and communication in the 21st century (Shetzer & Warschauer, 2000).

What Can We Glean From Second Language Acquisition Research?

There are seven hypotheses of second language acquisition (SLA), outlined by Chapelle (1998), that serve as reasonable guides to the informed application of computer-assisted language learning (CALL) practices in foreign language classrooms.

Making Key Linguistic Characteristics Salient

Technology provides us with access to multiple sources of target language data and empowers teachers to manipulate them in order to highlight features that are important for learners and thus to make learning more effective. For example, words, structures, and explanations of the second language on a teacher-made Web page can now be accompanied by audio glosses, translations, and real-time flashing to direct students' attention to a particular learning point.

Offering Modifications of Linguistic Input

Technology empowers teachers to modify input easier and faster by using repetition, providing nonverbal cues, and allowing students to change the input mode according to their individual preferences. This lowers their affective filter, makes the input more comprehensible, and motivates students—and don't forget that children enjoy technology! For example, Audio Portfolios (http://distancelearning.llc.msu.edu/audioportfolio) is a completely online tool developed by Michigan State University. It allows students to record video and audio with written commentary and share these with teachers and peers, and it provides a feedback function for the teacher.

Providing Opportunities for Comprehensible Output

Receiving more comprehensible input and giving students the opportunity to perform in a nonthreatening electronic environment would encourage and empower students to build their linguistic competence and achieve better results. For example, getting students to participate in an online chat discussion not only provides the teacher with a written record of the conversation but also allows the teacher to frame the discussion with the class as it transpires.

Providing Opportunities to Notice Errors

Teachers can also improve student self-monitoring skills because the electronic environment is less intimidating and provides cues for self-correction, as well as easy access to information. For example, students can participate in a blog or create one themselves. In doing so, they are making their language output public and thus developing an intrinsic motivation to self-reflect on what they write, leading to more conscious attempts to self-correct their work.

Providing Opportunities for Linguistic Output

Technology supports environments in which students can communicate more readily with native speakers anywhere in the world. For example, students can use both synchronous and asynchronous communication tools such as e-mail, online chats, and audioconferencing tools such as Skype (http://www.skype.com) and Gizmo (http://www.gizmoproject.com).

Supporting Modified Interaction in the Target Language

Even if a student is interacting only with the computer in the course of a specific task or activity, interaction is still happening. It can be accomplished simply through a mouse click. In addition, concepts such as sociocultural theory emphasize the importance of the social environment, in which learners use computers as a tool to enhance their language learning experience while interacting with peers and experts. The teacher can facilitate and support this interaction, for example, by enrolling students in and guiding them to become active participants in relevant Listservs.

Acting as a Participant in Second Language Tasks

Often, CALL tasks require second language learners to become actively engaged in the learning activity in order for the activity to be successfully negotiated. For example, using a wiki is a means of engaging students in the collaborative writing process.

How Can Information From Technology Research Inform Us?

By following the research on CALL, teachers can understand better how students and teachers perceive technology. Research also allows teachers to make better decisions about

♦ How to best make technology a constructive supplement in face-to-face classrooms

♦ How to best use technology in classrooms in terms of activities, teaching, and communication strategies

- How teaching approaches can be applied and implemented in both face-to-face and electronic environments

- How best to approach the use of technology and what to expect when engaging students in projects that use technology

- How to effectively engage students with different learning styles

Electronic Literacy—Do I Need It?

There are many types of literacy skills that we acquire throughout our lives. Most people think of reading or writing when they talk about literacy. However, there are many types of literacy skills that we acquire during our lifetime. Cooking, driving a car, knitting, and playing sports are all types of literacies. The ability to use technology is another type of literacy. It is often referred to as "electronic literacy" or "techoliteracy." In the schools of the 21st century, it is important for teachers to develop some type of literacy in using and applying technology in the classroom. The youth of today belong to the digital generation—students' lives are composed of iPods, digital recorders, PlayStations, computers, instant messaging—technology is their world. Thus, it is of consequence to teachers if they are to relate to their students in ways that the digital generation will understand—namely, with using technology.

What Type of 21st-Century Teacher Am I: Designer, Facilitator, or Manager?

The new role of the 21st-century teacher is to facilitate learning, to guide learners toward a common goal (Hunter, Bailey, & Taylor, 1995), and to support the development of lifelong learning skills. A successful facilitator needs to be a creative individual who is capable of leading learners through the learning experience and incorporates the skills of a good designer and manager. Can you be this kind of teacher?

References

Alavi, M., & Leidner, D. (2001). Research commentary: Technology-mediated learning—A call for greater depth and breadth of research. *Information Systems Research, 12*(1), 1–10.

American Council on the Teaching of Foreign Languages. (1996). *National standards for foreign language education.* Retrieved online January 16, 2003, from http://www.actfl.org/i4a/pages/index.cfm?pageid=3392.

Chapelle, C. A. (1998). Multimedia CALL: Lessons to be learned from research on instructed SLA. *Language Learning and Technology, 2*(1), 22–34.

Chapelle, C. A. (2001). *Computer applications in second language acquisition: Foundations for teaching, testing, and research.* New York: Cambridge University Press.

Dockstader, J. (1999). Teachers of the 21st century know the what, why, and how of technology integration. *T.H.E. Journal,* January 1999. Retrieved January 22, 2007, from http://www.thejournal.com/magazine/vault/A2084.cfm.

Egbert, J., Chao, C., & Hanson-Smith, E. (1999). Computer-enhanced language learning environments. In J. Egbert & E. Hanson-Smith (Eds.), *CALL environments: Research practice and critical issues* (pp. 1–13). Alexandria, VA: Teachers of English to Speakers of Other Languages.

Hunter, D., Bailey, A., & Taylor, B. (1995). *The art of facilitation: How to create group synergy.* Tucson, AZ: Fisher Books.

International Society for Technology in Education. (2000). *National educational technology standards.* Retrieved January 22, 2007, from http://cnets.iste.org/index.shtml.

Kanuka, H., & Anderson, T. (1999). Using constructivism in technology-mediated learning: Constructing order out of the chaos of the literature. *Radical Pedagogy, 1*(2). Retrieved January 22, 2007, from http://radicalpedagogy.icaap.org/content/issue1_2/.

Lantolf, J. P., & Appel, G. (1994). Theoretical framework: An introduction to Vygotskian approaches to second language research. In J. P. Lantolf & G. Appel (Eds.), *Vygostskian approaches to second language research* (pp. 1–32). Norwood, NJ: Ablex.

Mannetter, T. (2002). The natural approach: Technology in the second language classroom. *Teaching with Technology Today, 9*(2). Retrieved January 22, 2007, from http://www.uwsa.edu/ttt/articles/mannetter.htm.

Shetzer, H., & Warschauer, M. (2000). An electronic literacy approach to network language teaching. In M. Warschauer & R. Kern (Eds.), *Network-based language teaching: Concepts and practice* (pp. 171–185). New York: Cambridge University Press.

Vygotsky, L. S. (1978). *Mind in society: The development of higher psychological processes.* Cambridge, MA: Harvard University Press.

Warschauer, M. (1999). *Electronic literacies: Language, culture, and power in online education.* Mahwah, NJ: Lawrence Erlbaum.

3

Using Technology for Foreign Language Instruction: Creative Innovations, Research, and Applications

Tony Erben, Ruth Ban, Li Jin, Robert Summers, and Kristina Eisenhower

Throughout our collective 65 years as foreign language teachers and as members of a number of foreign language professional organizations, we have often gotten the impression that many foreign language teachers equate classroom success with quiet, serious, book-centered learning. However, an equal proportion of our colleagues believe the opposite is true, that is, they support interactive, engaged, student-centered, and most importantly, fun classroom lessons. Indeed, we all learned in our initial education methods courses that student motivation is a key factor in engaging students in learning. However, have you ever thought about the concept of fun as a teaching principle? What about a task type that underpins and facilitates fun as an ongoing motivational tool? We are talking about the use of technology as a classroom resource that has very sound theoretical justification in second language acquisition research, constructivism, cooperative learning, and sociocultural theory.

Unfortunately, in many classrooms, foreign language teachers view technology and its use as something that is tinkered with on a Friday afternoon or used as a reward when class conduct has been good. In this chapter, we want to reconceptualize the nature of technology and its place in the foreign language classroom. In effect, technology needs to be relocated as the fundamental basis for all of the things we do in the foreign-language classroom. The following sections discuss past and present issues concerning technology-enhanced education, what we can glean from research on computer-assisted language learning (CALL), what innovations in technology are beginning to emerge in education circles, and how these may influence what we do in our foreign language classrooms. First, however, let's look at the research before we cross the bridge into practice.

Historical Developments of CALL

By the early 1960s, universities had begun creating local area networks that allowed computers on campus to communicate with one another, affording a rapid exchange of information. Soon thereafter, educators became interested in using these networks for the purposes of language learning and teaching. In fact, Collett (1980) was one of the first to use his university mainframe computer to post grammar activities for his language students. Almost a decade later, Dunkel (1987) called for the use of computer-aided instruction as a more holistic, meaningful way to teach languages, in keeping with Canale and Swain's (1980) notion of communicative competence.

Since the early 1990s, research on computer-mediated communication (CMC) has examined how electronic media could be employed to enhance language learning (Beauvois, 1992; Chun, 1994; Chun & Plass, 2000; Kelm, 1992; Kern, 1992; Kern & Warschauer, 2000). Much of this research concluded that the use of an asynchronous discussion board (Beauvois, 1992; Chun, 1994; Kelm, 1992; Kern, 1992) promotes greater student participation, more requests for clarification and negotiation of meaning, and the use of more discourse structures. Other affective factors, such as lower anxiety (Kelm, 1992), increased motivation (Kern, 1995), and advantages for at-risk students (Beauvois, 1992) were also found in the use of synchronous chat. Similar studies pointed to the creation of a level playing field for students who are less likely to participate in a face-to-face classroom (Chun, 1994). In addition, some researchers (Chun, 1994; Kern, 1995; Sullivan & Pratt, 1996) began to question how language teaching and the role of the teacher are affected by the use of technology in the classroom.

To this end, researchers with more experience using technology in the foreign language classroom have begun to uncover other aspects of CMC that have a distinct impact on language teaching. Research shows that just using technology is not enough. There are certain conditions, such as appropriate time allowance and immediate feedback, that need to be met for technology to enhance language learning (Egbert & Hanson-Smith, 1999). Likewise, for learning benefits to be evident, teaching should combine media and interactivity (Pusack & Otto, 1997), that is, technology must be integrated into and woven throughout the curriculum, not merely added to existing classroom practices (Reigeluth, 1999). Most recently, research has examined the effects of negotiation of meaning (Fidalgo-Eick, 2001) and corrective feedback in synchronous CMC (Castañeda, 2005; Iwasaki & Oliver, 2003; Morris, 2002; Pellettieri, 2000) on the language learning process. Furthermore, it has been noted that technology can be used in two ways — either as a teacher or and as a tool (Levy, 1997). However, from an interactionist perspective of language learning, researchers view the computer as both a teacher and a tool and have demonstrated how computers can be used to provide input and opportunities for output, as well as feedback for learners (Ortega, 1997; Sotillo, 2000; Warschauer & Healey, 1998).

Now let's look at the implications of what we know from research on foreign language pedagogy.

The Impact of Technology on Classroom Practices

Authentic Materials in Foreign Language Classrooms

For decades, foreign language teaching and learning has been synonymous with drill-and-practice or drill-and-kill. In traditional foreign language classrooms, students were required to repeat and memorize information from artificially created language materials. Foreign language teachers who were actually interested in using authentic materials had to purchase them from overseas and wait for delivery through the postal service or bring them back from personal trips. In the 1970s, computer technologies were created and implemented for language teaching by way of computer laboratories. However, the use of these computer labs was still focused on rote memorization and drill-and-kill grammar exercises. It was not until the 1990s that we witnessed the burgeoning development of the Internet, which yielded unprecedented and exciting applications of computer technologies to foreign language teaching and learning. With unlimited and fast access to authentic materials from the target culture through the Internet, foreign language teachers are now able to create meaningful tasks and communicative settings in which learners have an authentic goal and audience. For example, to plan a weekend holiday in the Loire Valley, a student could visit the Web site of a French travel agency to obtain information about hotels, tours, transportation, and so forth. In addition, the Internet technologies (e.g., e-mail, online forums, and chat rooms) provide more opportunities for learners to have authentic conversations with native speakers in the target culture

(Warschauer & Kern, 2000), which enables language learning in a true cultural context. Direct access to the target language and culture also extends foreign language learning beyond the traditional classroom, where the teacher is the only knowledge transmitter. Students are now able to independently practice the foreign language in a real and meaningful environment.

Cooperative Learning in Foreign Language Classrooms

Cooperative learning is an instructional strategy that allows small, interactive groups of students to work collaboratively on meaningful tasks. When undertaking cooperative learning activities, students must rely on and help each other to accomplish certain tasks or achieve a common goal. This best (classroom) practice has gained considerable attention, particularly in the area of language learning. Both interactionist (Long, 1987) and sociocultural (Donato, 1989; Lantolf, 1994) researchers agree that collaboration and communication among learners help language learning to occur. For example, collaboration between a higher-level student and a lower-level student might allow scaffolding to take place. The interaction or collaboration between two learners helps mediate the development of the novice learner's language skills to an extent that would not be possible without expert help (Donato, 1989). Not only that, the higher-level student's knowledge and skills also are developed.

To that end, many researchers (e.g., Chun & Plass, 2000; Kern & Warschauer, 2000) have discovered that networking technologies provide an ideal medium for communication and can be used in foreign language classrooms to undertake cooperative learning activities. Examples include a foreign language group investigation project using instant messaging as the means of communication among all group members (Jin, 2004) or a cooperative jigsaw activity that uses chat rooms or e-mail exchanges, or perhaps pairs or small groups that collaborate by sharing one computer to participate in online discussions or electronic publishing.

Student-Centered Learning

The key to student-centered learning is the idea of *equity in education,* the belief that all students must be afforded a fair and equal opportunity to participate. In student-centered learning environments, classroom topics are relevant to students lives, needs, and interests, and students are actively engaged in creating, understanding, and connecting with knowledge (McCombs & Whistler, 1997). In student-centered classrooms, teachers share control, and students are allowed to explore, experiment, and discover on their own (Nunan, 1988). In this setting, computer technologies provide more venues for all students to be equally and actively engaged in language learning activities. For example, in a technology-enhanced foreign language classroom, the teacher is no longer the only information source. Equipped with Internet technologies, students have access to multiple sources of information in a variety of media. They are encouraged to explore, compare and contrast, and ultimately develop knowledge about the target language and culture. Additionally, online communication (e.g., discussion boards and chat rooms) enables multiple venues in which students can practice using the target language. For example, a well-designed electronic discussion board creates a less stressful setting, particularly for those who are shy in the regular classroom. In such a stress-free environment, students are more active and the teacher is less dominating, which ensures the equal participation of all students.

Through technology use, students are afforded more opportunities for reflective thinking about language learning and use. For example, when a learner composes an e-mail or elaborates a posting on a discussion board, there is time to consider both the meaning and the form of the language. As a result of this reflection, the learner is able to more appropriately apply learning strategies (Ulitsky, 2000). As students develop the ability to reflect on how they learn, they are able to expand and improve their learning capabilities (Oxford, 2000). Therefore, the systematic nature of the particular technology used in the classroom affords learners an opportunity to reflect and grow, both intellectually and metacognitively.

Learner Autonomy and Motivation

Learner autonomy is encouraged by allowing students to work independently, thereby engaging their full potential (Egbert & Hanson-Smith, 1999). Technology-enhanced settings such as discussion boards offer a protected, teacher-structured environment in which each student can stretch his or her potential and learn to take risks in a nonjudgmental context (Padr & Waxman, 1996). Within these disciplined environments, students feel supported and able to take the necessary risks in their learning, thus resulting in successful learning (Egbert, 2001). For example, a learner can take control of his or her language by referring to a dictionary or rewriting the message until he or she deems it satisfactory for posting. In addition, active learning, which puts the responsibility of organizing what is to be learned into the hands of the learners themselves, lends itself to a more diverse range of learning styles. An excellent example of autonomous, active learning is the International Tandem Network. Through this extensive e-mail network, language learners connect with native speakers of the target language to build pen pal relationships that not only foster autonomous learning but also cultivate literacy skills and cross-cultural understanding (http://www.slf.ruhr-un:-bochum.de/etandem/etindex-en.html).

Today students live in a world in which they are bombarded by multimedia messages that can facilitate their maneuvering through everyday life. Many students are naturally attracted to and motivated by activities that involve technology, especially in the educational arena. However, technology itself does not promote active learning, nor does technology use that is structured to mirror the teacher-fronted approach to language teaching and learning. Learners feel motivated when up-to-date and authentic materials are used to support learning (Dlaska, 2002) and when they have teachers who incorporate aspects of technology to scaffold their learning through the use of contextual cues such as images, icons, and audio and video elements (Chatel, 2002). For example, multimedia presentations delivered through the World Wide Web and online simulation programs provide easy-to-use and low-cost authentic information that students can explore and experience from their own individual perspective.

Risks and Rewards of CALL

The use of technology in the classroom can increase motivation, decrease anxiety, foster more student-centered activities, and provide students with authentic materials and audiences. Also, it can promote greater language production and a higher level of language sophistication, as well as enhance critical-thinking skills according to particular cultural contexts. However, even with all these benefits, the integration of technology into the foreign language classroom presents some challenges and possible pitfalls that teachers should be aware of. In the following sections, we interpret the results of the research for you.

Challenges of Technology Use in Foreign Language Classrooms

At the most basic level are technical difficulties, which frustrate teachers more than anything else. This could be as simple as a burned-out bulb or incompatible components in the computer projector or the cable to the laptop. More problematic situations might include broken links to desired Web sites or a server that is temporarily down. Without precaution, students can be easily upset or frustrated by these inconveniences. Though these situations might raise a teacher's level of frustration, as they say, don't throw out the technology with the bathwater. To reduce such avoidable frustrations, it is always a good idea to check the technology *before* you walk into your classroom!

There are also limitations that teachers should be familiar with. For example, because e-mail is asynchronous, an immediate answer or response is not expected. Synchronous communication tools, on the other hand, place more demand on students' language proficiency. Other considerations might include the quality of the software used. For example, the free software available on the Internet for videoconferencing often appears jumpy and pixilated online. However, it has been evidenced that students may be more receptive to seeing someone face while talking to him or her than just hearing a voice, no matter the clarity of the picture.

In keeping with students' needs, students should be trained in the use of these technologies before they are expected to carryout an assignment using them. Not only should students be trained in the use of a new program, they also should be advised of any rules surrounding its use. For example, when initiating a discussion board in class, the first step would be to have students introduce themselves and respond to at least one posting by one of their peers. This procedure should first be explained and then modeled to the class. If this type of training is not provided, students may experience stress that distances them from the technologies being used. When used properly, however, the benefits of technology seem to far outweigh the risks.

Another challenge that may concern foreign language teachers is classroom control. In a traditional classroom, the teacher is the center of teaching and learning. Thus, it is easy for the teacher to know where students are and how much progress students need to achieve. However, both the teacher and students may feel lost in a poorly designed technology-enhanced classroom. For example, students may visit irrelevant Web sites when they are asked to search for important information about the target culture. Without necessary constraints and explicit rules, the teacher may have no control over which Web sites students access and what is achieved by the end of class. Therefore, to ensure the optimal use of technologies in a foreign language classroom, a pedagogically sound teaching plan is necessary. Both the teacher and students should be aware of the class objectives and general procedures for carrying out online activities.

Best Practices for Using Technology in Foreign Language Classrooms

In order to bridge theoretical and practical considerations, it is important for language teachers to be able to apply research findings to their everyday practice. This section sets forth specific suggestions for integrating technology into curriculum development and teaching materials. In addition, it offers ideas for the appropriate development and use of teaching materials, as well as practical classroom applications. These *do's* of technology use will provide a strong basis for language teachers to integrate technology into the classroom.

Know Your Students

To successfully integrate technology into daily classroom learning, begin by getting to know your students' skill levels. A most serviceable manner in which to do this is by conducting a needs assessment of their computer skills. Teachers can construct a short survey or adapt one found online (see http://www.mccsc.edu/survey.html). The results of the needs assessment will facilitate the development of appropriate lessons that address both the students technology skills and language learning abilities. However, it is important to note that we cannot expect students to learn both technology and a foreign language at the same time. Teachers should be prepared to monitor students work on classroom-based tasks and support students use of technology.

Choosing Materials

When developing original materials, create tasks that fit students' learning potential and fit appropriately with the technology (Chapelle, 2001). For example, for students who are Internet savvy, assigning a WebQuest on a topic they are familiar with can motivate them to use the language they are learning to complete a task that is based on authentic materials (Egbert & Hanson-Smith, 1999; Egbert, Paulus, & Nakamichi, 2002; Warschauer & Healey, 1998). This type of purposeful and contextualized material allows students to apply their knowledge of the world to their language learning tasks. For novice language learners, choosing technology that supports text with images such as photos, graphs, or charts is highly advisable. Additionally, teachers can create materials that support and advance students development of electronic literacies. For example, using the Internet to research as well as write a report provides multiple sources of information that motivate students to learn more about the topic.

Students Working With Technology

One of the biggest challenges of integrating technology with classroom tasks is the shift in the role of the teacher (Chun, 1994; Kern, 1995; Sullivan & Pratt, 1996). Technology-enhanced classrooms have been found to promote discovery learning, learner autonomy, and learner-centeredness. One avenue toward activating these skills is for teachers to allow students to work collaboratively in pairs or small groups in which they can engage in interactive problem-solving or cooperative projects.

Language Use

Creating an authentic language context by modeling and encouraging the use of the target language while working with technology in a classroom setting has been found to be complicated because technology use implies more autonomous learning or self-directed learning. However, research findings indicate that students tend to use the target language more if the teacher models and supports language use.

Technologies on the Horizon and Their Potential Impact

Technology changes at such a quick pace that at times it takes our breath away — no sooner have we bought a new laptop than it has been superceded by a newer, faster, brighter edition. In this section, we would like to introduce you to a number of emerging technologies that have yet to leave their mark on the way we conceive of pedagogy in our foreign language classrooms. We have chosen the following technologies for their latent prospect in facilitating foreign language learning. Ultimately, it is *you* who will choose to tinker with these new technology toys and include them in your classroom practices.

Mobile Learning: Cell Phones, PDAs, and iPods

Mobile learning is the ability to take the learning medium with you anytime and anywhere in order to improve or master a particular skill. In the area of foreign language learning, mobile materials can be constructed by teachers and reused in different classes to maximize resources. Clearly, the Internet is the means of distribution for these materials, and the most common way of connecting to the Internet is with a personal computer. However, new technologies are allowing us to connect to the Web from a variety of places. These new Web-enabled technologies include cell phones, personal digital assistants (PDAs), and iPods. These devices and their potential for mobile learning are particularly appealing and advantageous to today's teachers and students because most educators and older learners maintain busy schedules that are replete with work and school activities.

Fortunately, many schools and universities are now equipped with wireless access points. These wireless networks permit anyone with a wireless-equipped device to connect to the Internet. Once connected, students can browse Web sites, listen to streaming audio, watch streaming video, download podcasts, or communicate with others through instant messaging services or chat programs.

The current Web-enabled cell phones and PDAs are precursors of technology that promises to be even more compact and powerful. Despite their minute size, there has been substantial growth in the storage capacity, intuitiveness, and usefulness of these appliances. Therefore, it can be said that the future of mobile learning, which will allow students to experience new levels of interactivity and engagement by accessing the Web anywhere, is embodied in these devices. In the following sections, we address specific technologies that we feel are of particular interest to foreign language educators.

Podcasts

The term *podcast* is a combination of two words: *pod* is from iPod, the portable audio player made by Apple that plays audio files, and *cast* comes from roadcast, to make something widely known, as in a program that is transmitted to a large audience. Podcasts are audio recordings that range in quality from very polished and professional to quirky and homemade. The creation of podcasts is relatively easy using free software that can be downloaded from the Internet. However, it is important to note that although podcasting is a technology that was started by Apple enthusiasts, you do not have to own an iPod or Apple computer to listen to or create a podcast. Anyone with a computer and an Internet connection can participate in podcasting. The simplest way to listen to podcast serializations is to download iTunes, which is free, and then, through iTunes, search for your podcast.

Podcasts and Interactivity

Though some critics have posited that podcasts are limited in their usefulness in the classroom because of their lack of interactivity, they have only seen them used in traditional ways. The original purpose of podcasts was passive listening to audio files. However, podcasts today are highly interactive and actively engage students in their own learning. To illustrate the interactivity of a podcast used in foreign language learning, consider the following example:

A teacher creates and posts a podcast in French that the students are asked to download and listen to. The podcast process begins by asking students to listen to a short story about a young man who has just arrived in the Ivory Coast; however, the story quickly changes once the scene has been set and the characters established. The student is confronted with choices to make and must interact with the technology to finish the story. For example, the listener must decide by what means the young man will get to his hotel. In the story, a stranger offers him a ride to his hotel, or he has the option to take a taxi. At this point, if the student chooses the taxi option, he or she is directed to listen to another podcast that continues the story from the taxi ride. If the student decides that the young man should accept the stranger offer, he or she will be directed to listen to a different podcast that continues the story based on that decision. This interactivity continues throughout the podcast, with a variety of options and paths offered to the learner.

Research regarding both synchronous and asynchronous communication among students in foreign language classes and students in the target culture has shown that such communications hastens the development of language acquisition (Belz, 2002). Moreover, students who communicate electronically generally produce a greater quantity of language that is more complex than their spoken language (Kern, 1995). Beauvois (1992) and Kelm (1992) both posit that this is because students have some level of anonymity in a networked computerized environment. Though constructing a podcast does not offer the same type of anonymity as text-based communication, the ability to edit contributes to students feelings of comfort while using the language. Podcasts can be used in the same fashion to produce the same results. For example, students can communicate with peers in another country by creating their own podcasts. In turn, their counterparts can respond by creating a new podcast.

Pros and Cons of Podcasting

There are several advantages to the use of podcasts in educational settings. First, most students already have some understanding of the technology used to listen to podcasts. That is, they are familiar with the downloading process because many have downloaded music and video from the Internet to their personal computers. Additionally, instead of a portable compact disc player or cassette player, many students own and carry MP3 players with them on a daily basis. Portability is another distinct advantage of learning through podcasts. For example, a student who has missed a class would be able to listen to the classroom discussion at their convenience, which could also act as an adjunct to the classroom interaction. Finally, although the file type that Apple sometimes uses in iTunes is compatible only with iPods, this does not mean the only way to listen to a podcast is to have an iPod. Apple files (.acc) can easily be converted to play on any MP3 player with the appropriate file conversion software.

An unfortunate attribute of podcasts is their size. These files are sometimes an hour or more in length, creating files that can be quite large. Another disadvantage of podcasts is the potential for poor production quality, in that some podcasts have shown evidence of using faulty equipment and abrupt editing. At the present time, making a podcast is not necessarily intuitive for the user. We hope that this will change in the near future.

Blogs

The term *blog* is short for *weblog,* a term coined by Jorn Barger in 1997 to describe Web sites that are updated continuously. Other derivatives of this term include *blogsphere,* which describes a dynamic network of blogs (Blood, 2000) and *blogger,* which is the author of the weblog. Though there is no agreement as to a single definition of a blog, Ward (2004) offers a working definition that describes the general concept: A blog is a Web site that is updated regularly and organized chronologically, with the most current entry listed first. It can be compared to a type of interactive public journal. A blog is similar to an e-mail message in that any reader can reply to it, yet it is different because it is published to the Internet. Often, readers' replies contain a Web address that links to additional information. Also, a blog is less intrusive than e-mails because the reader chooses to visit the blogger site instead of receiving a myriad of e-mails. It is similar to an online forum. Moreover, old postings are archived and can be accessed by readers.

Generally, blogs chronicle an individual experience in some aspect of their life. For example, several blogs detail the differences between the writer's home country and the United

States. These blogs explain the sacrifices and adaptations that their authors have made during their time away from their home. One of the most well-known bloggers is Salam Pax, an Iraqi who published a blog that described his lived experiences during his country's invasion and the following occupation. This famous blogger brought the notion of blogging into the spotlight and highlighted the fact that anyone with a computer and Internet connection can publish their thoughts.

Blogs and Writing

There are well-documented findings that students are more motivated to produce written work and strive for better quality when they are provided with an authentic audience (Grabe & Kaplan, 1996; Mendon & Johnson, 1994; Mittan, 1989; Tsui & Ng, 2000; Warschauer, 1998). A distinct advantage of student-created blogs is increased motivation and desire to produce quality work. Furthermore, writing for Web publication ensures a multicultural audience that may interact with students by offering comments and suggestions concerning the content of the messages. This quasi-peer revision promotes student reflection and engenders a feeling of ownership of the blog.

Just as journal writing is an iterative process, the upkeep of a blog requires the same revisions and modifications that illustrate the process of writing as ongoing. Blogging requires the author to continually publish, that is, there is constant revising and reflecting to create a finished product. It becomes a collection of student work that can be assessed holistically, much like a portfolio.

Research has shown that students are less likely to have anxiety when they are communicating in a computer-mediated environment (Bradley & Lomicka, 2000; Doughty & Long, 2003; Warschauer 1998). They also tend to produce more complex and sophisticated language in such an environment (Beauvois, 1992; Chun & Plass, 1995; Kelm, 1992). Additionally, the anonymity of publishing on the Internet provides a low-risk distribution medium that provides learners with a platform on which they can experiment with the language and increase their level of confidence.

Blogs and Reading

As previous research has shown, access to the Internet provides both students and teachers with a multitude of authentic language materials. This virtual environment includes online newspapers, menus, shopping sites, videos, and blogs. Reading blogs written by others who share the same interests can be particularly appealing to students. The dynamic reading that a blog offers is much more meaningful than the static reading found in traditional print media, as it cognitively engages students when the public discussion concerns their own personal experiences (Crawford, Marx, & Krajcik, 1999). Moreover, this type of reading serves the important purpose of introducing the language learner to the target society and helps build a community of learners (Preece, 2000).

Reading blogs can also develop critical-thinking skills. The ability to critically evaluate electronically published information is paramount to the successful use of the Web, and teachers should ensure that students know how to distinguish reputable materials from questionable ones (Warschauer, 1998). In other words, teachers should remind students of the potential fallibility of information presented on the Web and equip students with the tools to critically analyze these materials.

Blog Activities

Reading blogs gives students an opportunity to correspond with native speakers and experiment with the language. Reading and responding to a blog is an interactive endeavor for students, as they become engaged in reading others' replies to their posted comments and actively follow hyperlinks to explore sites related to the topic they are reading about.

Blogs can also be used in conjunction with other technologies. For example, students might be asked to complete a WebQuest and then post their findings to a blog; other classmates might respond to the blog and offer suggestions or comments, prompting the author to reflection on his or her original writing. Students can also work together to create a blog that is pertinent to a current class activity. This type of extension reinforces new material and expands previous knowledge.

Additionally, blogs are an excellent way to showcase and assess student-created materials, as is done with electronic portfolios. There are many free sites on which students can post their writing and read what others have posted. Examples include http://www.blogger.com, http://www.spaces.msn.com, and http://www.blogdrive.com. These sites have additional features that allow bloggers to upload photos, add interactivity, and provide easy navigation for readers to view the newest blog installment.

Not only can students use a weblog as a reflective tool, but also teachers can use this reflective tool. For example, an educator could start a blog about a new unit introduced in class, post a collection of activities or tasks that worked well or ones that did not, or perhaps exchange experiences and advice with other teachers. Given the technological nature of blogging, it is no surprise that there are numerous examples of blogs that detail teachers experiences using computers and other technologies in the classroom.

We refer you to a wonderful chapter written by Tekiner and Cresswell, which appears in the online extension of this book. Called *Blogs for Language Teachers,* it can be found at http://utweb.ut.edu/Faculty/terben/CALL.html.

Wikis

A *wiki* is a collaborative, open-editing Internet tool that was developed by Ward Cunningham in 1994. This tool allows users to co-create and co-edit Web site content using any Web browser (Leuf & Cunningham, 2001). Since its debut in the early 1990s, the wiki has gained significant popularity as a way to facilitate computer-supported collaborative learning, usually in a writing application. An excellent example of wiki technology can be found at http://wikipedia.org.

Participation in a wiki generally takes one of two forms. The first is a document mode, in which all contributors can create documents. In this mode, each participant can anonymously edit or replace documents that others have posted, thereby transforming the document as multiple and changing authors comment and create newer iterations of the same documents. The resulting piece is compiled and published to represent the shared knowledge or beliefs of all the contributors (Leuf & Cunningham, 2001). The second wiki mode is known as a thread mode. In this style of wiki, contributors are expected to sign their posted messages, and others respond with their own signed commentary while leaving the original message unedited. To that end, the thread mode can be thought of as a conversation or discussion among participants, whereas the document mode reflects more of a final thesis or dissertation from the contributors (Leuf & Cunningham, 2001).

What is most important to foreign language teachers who have an interest in collaborative learning through writing is that wikis can use multiple languages, so people around the world can contribute to wiki sites in their own languages. In fact, using wikis for second language writing activities has become increasingly popular as a motivating medium for students. Traditional writing assignments require learners to individually compose and edit their own drafts, but in wiki writing, multiple rather than individual authors are encouraged to compose, rewrite, and openly edit multiple texts at any time. In the wiki medium, the authorship and ownership of the text are shifted from a single person to the whole class, blurring the distinction between the author, the reviewer, the audience, and the evaluator. The use of wikis in a classroom setting promotes peer interaction and augments the sharing and construction of knowledge and expertise among a group of learners. This knowledge sharing and co-construction consequently empowers students and leads to learning autonomy (Myers, 1991).

To establish a wiki site for your own writing class, you can apply for a free account through a wiki hosting site, such as http://www.seedwiki.com, or visit http://en.wikipedia.org/wiki/List_of_wiki_farms to search for more free wiki hosting services. Once you have set up an account, you will be directed to create a name and description for your wiki site and define its major features, such as language, topic, posting protocols, and so forth. After you have created a wiki site, you can invite your students into the wonderful world of writing with wikis!

Again, we refer you to a great chapter replete with classroom activities written by Jane Harvey. It can be found at http://utweb.ut.edu/Faculty/terben/CALL.html.

Simulation Gaming

Marc Prensky, a world-renowned writer in the field of digital gaming, has characterized the schoolchildren of today as the digital generation. This idea is based on the key premise that these learners have changed in some fundamentally important ways. That is, the bulk of the students in schools today born after 1990 are, in a very real intellectual sense, not the same as the students of the past (Prensky, 2001).

Prensky (2001) explains that the students of today have grown up with computers, PlayStations, and Game Boys. With radical changes and innovations in technology such the pocket calculator, the laptop computers, digital cameras and videos, the compact disc, the wireless telephone, the Internet, the MP3 player, and so on, children recreational experiences in the last 20 years have shifted dramatically. Today youth, in elementary school through college, travel with their own personal Game Boys, Handycams, cell phones, portable CD and MP3 players, pagers, laptops, and Internet connections. Statistics show that, each day, the average teenager in America watches more than three hours of television, spends a half hour on the Internet, and plays an hour and a half of video games. Altogether, these students watch more than 20,000 hours of television, play more than 10,000 hours of video games, see hundreds of movies in theaters and on video, and are exposed to more than 400,000 television commercials, adding up to tens of millions of images. Clearly, these kids are the digital generation (Prensky, 2001).

For foreign language teachers, one of the biggest problems in language learning whether it takes place in a classroom, online, or from a distance is keeping students motivated to stick with the learning process. Why is motivation so hard to maintain? For one, all learning requires effort. What motives do our foreign language students have for learning the Spanish, French, German, or Latin material presented to or required of them? There are, of course, students who learn for the sake and joy of learning. Unfortunately, we see this only rarely. Realistically, students' motives for foreign language learning are a mixture of intrinsic goals and extrinsic rewards, combined with psychological factors such as fear and the need to please. If strong enough, these motives can keep the students on the right path.

How effective will these forms of motivation be in the future? In the world of education, providing motivation is one of the teacher's traditional roles. However, Prensky (2001) says that computer and video games are so engaging and education is often so *un*engaging not because that is the natural state of things or the nature of the beast. The reason computer games are so captivating is that the primary objective of game designers is to keep the user engaged. They need to keep that player coming back, day after day, for 30, 60, even 100 or more hours, so that the person feels as if he or she has gotten some value for his or her money (and, in the case of online games, keeps paying). That is their measure of success.

Previous research that has investigated the nature and use of games and play has identified two common elements in the notion of play. The first is that playful activities elicit involvement. The second is that they also provide pleasure. Starbuck and Webster (1991) have discovered some common characteristics among people who play:

♦ People play at work to seek competence, stimulation, challenge, or reinforcement.

♦ People who perform very playful tasks enjoy what they are doing. When they judge those activities as appropriate, they switch to them readily and try to continue doing them.

♦ They tend to concentrate more and increase their persistence.

♦ They become less aware of the passage of time and are reluctant to change activities.

- They become so absorbed that they may neglect other things, such as long-term goals, nonplayful tasks, and social relations.

- Their learning is enhanced because the pleasure and involvement of playful activities induces them to expend time and effort.

- Through different forms of play, they broaden their behavioral repertoire incrementally, discover or invent radically new behaviors, and polish their existing skills through repetitive practice.

- Playful tasks foster creativity. If the playful tasks are new ones, they will put a great deal of effort into learning them and exploring them, usually trying to control their own learning.

The Horizon Report, a collaborative effort between the New Media Consortium and the Educause Learning Initiative, is an annual "think-tank," research-oriented effort that seeks to identify and describe emerging technologies likely to have a large impact on teaching, learning or creative expression within educational contexts. In its 2006 report, four major trends were identified that were perceived to reflect significant changes in attitudes toward technology and communication in education circles. These trends were (a) the widespread acceptance of dynamic knowledge creation and social computing tools and processes; (b) the recognition of mobile and personal technology as a delivery platform for services of all kinds; (c) the expectation by educational consumers to receive individualized services, tools, and experiences, as well as more open access to media, knowledge, and information; and (d) the acknowledgement that collaboration across the range of educational activities is critical, including intra- and interinstitutional activities of any size or scope. Within the above trends, the 2006 report (p. 5) details six technologies that are making significant inroads into classrooms across the United States.

- *Social Computing* is fast replacing face-to-face meetings with virtual collaborative tools;

- *Personal Broadcasting* has its genesis in text-based messaging. Blogger.com enables video and audio broadcasting (vlogging) of MP3 files that can link with Itunes for serialization;

- *Phones & PDAs in Pockets* is an on-demand means to access educational content;

- *Augmented Reality and Enhanced Visualization* allow large data sets to be represented in 3D;

- *Context-Aware Environments* give rise to intelligent rooms that respond to voice commands; and

- *Educational Gaming* has prompted renewed research interest into engagement theory, the effect of using games in practice and the structure of cooperation in game play.

What does all of this have to do with foreign language learning? Everything! To return to what we said in the introduction to this chapter fun and games promote motivation. Currently, there is ample research to suggest that games and more recently, digital games provide learners with a unique set of stimuli that promote learning in many different areas, such as cognitive, social, and physical dimensions. Fortunately, we have now entered a time during which teachers are able to use their own templates to create their own unique and fun digital games specifically for foreign language learners. For more information on the use of games in the foreign language classroom, visit any of the Web sites listed at the end of this chapter: for a resource on how particular games promote specific learning activities and skills-based learning in students, see Erben's (2006) thorough (though not yet exhaustive) chart in Appendix B of this chapter. These materials should help you get in the game and start playing!

Conclusion

A wide variety of technologies are pervasive in our daily life. As we have seen, researchers and practitioners have recognized that technologies provide great potential for foreign language teaching and learning. In this chapter, we have only scratched the surface of the many activities that can be enhanced by the integration of these technologies and how and when they can be used in particular classroom settings. As with any new pedagogical method or technique, cautions on practical the use of technology, in general, are also provided to help prevent potential drawbacks inherent in these technologies. We expect you now have a broader exposure to the multitude of technologies available and will attempt to actively integrate some of the technologies introduced here, as well as develop and share your own creative and un innovations and applications of technology use in the foreign language classroom.

APPENDIX A
WEB SITES FOR CREATING GAMES[1]

♦ Puzzles: http://www.quia.com, http://www.puzzlemaker.com, http://web.uvic.ca/hrd/hotpot/

♦ Language games from Link to Learning: http://www.linktolearning.com/language.htm

♦ Quest Atlantis (three-dimensional multiuser environment for teaching and learning): http://atlantis.crlt.indiana.edu/start/

♦ Education Arcade (consortium of game designers that promotes educational uses of gaming): http://www.educationarcade.org/

♦ Gaming to Learn workshop (sponsored by Mexcia X): http://mediax.stanford.edu/news/sep05_03.html

♦ Serious Games Initiative: http://www.seriousgames.org/

♦ Serious Games Wiki: http://www.coe.ilstu.edu/rpriegle/eaf228/

♦ EAF 228 education course (structured to appear like a video game, by Rod Riegle): http://www.coe.ilstu.edu/rpriegle/eaf228/

♦ Social Impact Games: http://www.socialimpactgames.com/

♦ Serious Games Summit: http://www.seriousgamessummit.com/

♦ ELLS Project (joint American and Chinese language learning project using gaming): http://www.seriousgamessummit.com/

♦ Simulation and gaming issues in language learning: http://sag.sagepub.com/content/v0133/issue2/

♦ Simulation as a language learning tactic: http://www.languages.dk/methods/documents/Simulation_Manual.pdf

♦ ICONS experimental Web-based simulation project: http://www.icons.umd.edu/

♦ MMOG Research links to papers by Constance Steinkueler on multiplayer online games: https://mywebspace.wisc.edu/steinkuehler/web/mmogresearch.html

1   Adapted from Godwin-Jones (2005).

APPENDIX B

What comes automatically to mind when one thinks of the notion of "game" is something akin to a board-game such as monopoly or a virtual-game such as played on a Playstation or a Gameboy. However, there is more to game play than one may first assume and perceiving games as something akin to an online activity or a board game may be a very constraining and narrow perspective. Programs in game design are emerging in universities across the United States. They typically draw on the fields of psychology, cognitive science, computer science, education, and instructional design. The complexity of this new discipline is reflected in the array of gaming types that are currently being investigated for their educational potential. These include simulation games that mimic real-world processes, virtual environments that offer visually rich theme-independent settings, social-cooperative games that enable multi-player role-playing and alternative reality games that involve game play over time and space, often taking weeks or months to complete.

Board Games	# of Players	Functions That Can Be Practiced	Language That Can Be Practiced
Monopoly	3–6	Asking, making requests, buying/selling	Numbers, directions, city establishments
Battleship	2	Asking	Numbers, letters
Snakes & Ladders	2–6	Expressing opinions	Numbers
Guess Who	2	Expressing opinions, asking	Adjectives, body parts
Twister	2–4	Giving commands, rejecting and accepting advice	Body parts
Operation	2	Rejecting and accepting advice	Body parts
Clue	2–8	Expressing opinions	Family names, adjectives, household objects
Yahtzee/Boggle	2–6	Letters, guessing	Vocabulary expansion
Scrabble	2–4	Letters, guessing	Vocabulary expansion
Payday/Life	2–6	Expressing compliments	Professions, accounting, money, hobbies, education
Jeopardy		Asking	Interrogatives, word order
Sorry	2–4	Expressing opinions, asking	Time
Trivial Pursuit	2–6	Asking	Any topic, reading
Uno	2–4	Expressing	Numbers
Concentration	2–3	Expressing	Any topic

Digital Games	Gaming Type	Functions That Can Be Practiced	Nature of Language Practice
Second Life	Simulation	Judging, analyzing, explaining, expressing	Synchronous interaction, pragmatics, sociolinguistics
Sims	Simulation		
Operator's Side	Virtual environment	Expressing processes, describing	Synchronous interaction, pragmatics, sociolinguistics
ActiveWorlds.com	Virtual environment		
ThinkingWorlds	Virtual environment		
Environmental Detectives	Alternative reality	Asking, accepting, refusing	Written and spoken discourse
Seaman	Alternative reality		
Games2train	Social-cooperative	All possible functions can be practiced depending on how the "gaming environment" is set up	Reading, writing, listening speaking, culture, and grammar
Cybertrain	Social-cooperative		

References

Beauvois, M. H. (1992). Computer-assisted classroom discussion in the foreign language classroom: Conversation in slow motion. *Foreign Language Annals, 25*(5), 455–63.

Belz, J. A. (2002). Social dimensions of telecollaborative foreign language study. *Language Learning and Technology, 6*(1), 60–1.

Blood, R. (2000, September 7). *Weblogs: A history and perspective.* Retrieved January 23, 2007, from http://www.rebeccablood.net/essays/weblog_history.html.

Bradley, T., & Lomicka, L. (2000). A case study of learner interaction in technology-enhanced language learning environments. *Journal of Educational Computing Research, 22*(3), 347–68.

Canale, M., & Swain, M. (1980). Theoretical bases of communicative approaches to second-language teaching and testing. *Applied Linguistics, 1*(1), 1–7.

Castañeda, M. (2005). *Corrective feedback in online asynchronous and synchronous environments in Spanish as a foreign (SFL) classes.* Unpublished doctoral dissertation, University of South Florida, Tampa.

Chapelle, C. A. (2001). *Computer applications in second language acquisition: Foundations for teaching, testing, and research.* New York: Cambridge University Press.

Chatel, R. G. (2002). New technology, new literacy. *New England Reading Association Journal, 38*(3), 45–9.

Chun, D. M. (1994). Using computer networking to facilitate the acquisition of interactive competence. *System, 22*(1), 17–31.

Chun, D. M., & Plass, J. L. (1995). Project CyberBuch: A hypermedia approach to computer-assisted language learning. *Journal of Educational Multimedia and Hypermedia, 4*(1), 95–116.

Chun, D. M., & Plass, J. L. (2000). Networked multimedia environments for second language acquisition. In M. Warschauer, & R. Kern, (Eds.), *Network-based language teaching: Concepts and practice* (pp. 151 70). New York: Cambridge University Press.

Collett, M. J. (1980). Examples of applications of computers to modern language study 1: The step-wise development of programs in reading, grammar, and vocabulary. *System, 8*(3), 195–204.

Crawford, B., Marx, R., & Krajcik, J. (1999). Developing collaboration in a middle school project-based science classroom. *Science Education, 83*(6), 701–23.

Dlaska, A. (2002). Sites of construction: Language learning, multimedia, and the international engineer. *Computers and Education, 39*(2), 129–43.

Donato, R. (1989). Beyond group: A psycholinguistic rationale for collective activity in second-language learning. *Dissertation Abstracts International, 49*(12), 3701-A. (UMI No. DA8904593)

Doughty, C. J., & Long, M. H. (2003). Optimal psycholinguistic environments for distance foreign language learning. *Language Learning and Technology, 7*(3), 50–80.

Dunkel, P. (1987). Computer-assisted instruction (CAI) and computer-assisted language learning (CALL): Past dilemmas and future prospects for audible CALL. *Modern Language Journal, 71*(3), 250–60.

Egbert, J. (2001). Active learning through computer-enhanced activities. *Teaching English With Technology, 1*(3). Retrieved January 24, 2007, from http://www.iatefl.org.pl/sig/call/j_article3.htm.

Egbert, J. (2002). A project for everyone: English language learners and technology in content-area classrooms. *Learning and Leading with Technology, 29*(8), 36 –41.

Egbert, J., & Hanson-Smith, E. (1999). *CALL environments: Research, practice, and critical issues.* Alexandria, VA: Teachers of English to Speakers of Other Languages.

Egbert, J., Paulus, T. M., & Nakamichi, Y. (2002). The impact of CALL instruction on classroom computer use: A foundation for rethinking technology in teacher education. *Language Learning and Technology, 6*(3), 108–26.

Egbert, J., & Simich-Dudgeon, C. (2001). Providing support for non-native learners of English in the social studies classroom. *The Social Studies, 92*(1), 22–5.

Erben, T. (2006). Technology and the use of the "game" as an activity in the foreign language classroom: Overview and what research says. *Florida Foreign Language Journal, 1*(3), 10–23.

Fidalgo-Eick, M. (2001). Synchronous on-line negotiation of meaning by intermediate learners of Spanish. *Dissertation Abstracts International, 62*(3), 992. (UMI No. DA3009591)

Godwin-Jones, R. (2005). Messaging, gaming, peer-to-peer sharing: Language learning strategies and tools for the millennial generation. *Language Learning and Technology 9*(1), 17–22.

Grabe, W., & Kaplan, R. B. (1996). *Theory and practice of writing: An applied linguistic perspective.* New York: Longman.

Greenfield, P. M. (1984). *Mind and media: The effects of television, video games, and computers.* Cambridge, MA: Harvard University Press

Iwasaki, J., & Oliver, R. (2003). Chat-line interaction and negative feedback. *Australian Review of Applied Linguistics, 17,* 60–3.

Jin, L. (2004, October). *Instant messenger-mediated intercultural learning.* Paper presented at the annual meeting of the Second Language Research Forum, State College, PA.

Kelm, O. R. (1992). The use of synchronous computer networks in second language instruction: A preliminary report. *Foreign Language Annals, 25*(5), 441–53.

Kern, R. G. (1992). Teaching second language texts: Schematic interaction, affective response and the directed reading-thinking activity. *Canadian Modern Language Review, 48*(2), 307–25.

Kern, R. G. (1995). Restructuring classroom interaction with networked computers: Effects on quantity and characteristics of language production. *Modern Language Journal, 79*(4), 457–76.

Kern, R., & Warschauer, M. (2000). Introduction: Theory and practice of networked-based language teaching. In M. Warschauer, & R. Kern (Eds.), *Network-based language teaching: Concepts and practice.* Retrieved August 3, 2007, from http://www.gse.uci.edu/faculty/markw/nlolt-intro.html.

Lantolf, J. P. (1994). Sociocultural theory and second language learning: Introduction to the special issue. *Modern Language Journal, 78*(4), 418–20.

Lee, L. (1998). Going beyond classroom learning: Acquiring cultural knowledge via on-line newspapers and intercultural exchanges via on-line chatrooms. *CALICO Journal, 16*(2), 101–20.

Leuf, B., & Cunningham, W. (2001). *The Wiki way: Quick collaboration on the Web.* Boston: Addison-Wesley.

Levy, M. (1997). *Computer-assisted language learning: Context and conceptualization.* New York: Oxford University Press.

Long, M. H. (1987). The experimental classroom. *Annals of the American Academy of Political and Social Science, 490,* 97–109.

McCombs, B. L., & Whistler, J. S. (1997). *The learner-centered classroom and school: Strategies for increasing student motivation and achievement.* San Francisco: Jossey-Bass.

Mendon, C. O., & Johnson, K. E. (1994). Peer review negotiations: Revision activities in ESL writing instruction. *TESOL Quarterly, 28*(4), 745–69.

Mittan, R. (1989). The peer review process: Harnessing students communicative power. In D. M. Johnson & D. H. Roen (Eds.), *Richness in writing: Empowering ESL students* (pp. 207–19). New York: Longman.

Morris, F. A. (2002). Negotiation moves and recasts in relation to error types and learner repair in the foreign language classroom. *Foreign Language Annals, 35*(4), 395–404.

Myers, J. (1991). Cooperative learning in heterogeneous classes. *Cooperative Learning, 11*(4).

Nunan, D. (1988). *The learner-centered curriculum; A study in second language teaching.* New York: Cambridge University Press.

Ortega, L. (1997). Processes and outcomes in networked classroom interaction: Defining the research agenda for L2 computer-assisted classroom discussion. *Language Learning and Technology, 1*(1), 82–93.

Oxford, R. (2000). Language learning styles and strategies: Concepts and relationships. *Modern Language Journal, 78*(X), 271–78.

Padr, Y. N., & Waxman, H. C. (1996). Improving the teaching and learning of English language learners through instructional technology. *International Journal of Instructional Media, 23*(4), 341–54.

Pellettieri, J. (2000). Negotiation in cyberspace. In M. Warschauer & R. Kern (Eds.), *Network-based language teaching: Concepts and practice* (pp. 59 6). New York: Cambridge University Press.

Preece, J. (2000). *Online communities: Designing usability, supporting sociability.* Chichester, UK: Wiley.

Prensky, M. (2001). *Digital game-based learning.* New York: McGraw-Hill.

Pusack, J. P., & Otto, S. K. (1997). Taking control of multimedia. In M. D. Bush & R. M. Terry (Eds.), *Technology-enhanced language learning* (pp. 1 6). Lincolnwood, IL: National Textbook.

Reigeluth, C. M. (Ed.). (1999). *Instructional-design theories and models: Vol. II. A new paradigm of instructional theory.* Mahwah, NJ: Lawrence Erlbaum.

Sotillo, S. M. (2000). Discourse functions and syntactic complexity in synchronous and asynchronous communication. *Language Learning and Technology, 4*(1), 82–119.

Starbuck, W. H., & Webster, J. (1991). When is play productive? *Accounting, Management, and Information Technology 1*(1), 71–80.

Sullivan, N., & Pratt, E. (1996). A comparative study of two ESL writing environments: A computer-assisted classroom and a traditional oral classroom. *System, 24*(4), 491–501.

Tsui, A. B. M., & Ng, M. (2000). Do secondary L2 writers benefit from peer comments? *Journal of Second Language Writing, 9*(2), 147–70.

Ulitsky, H. (2000). Language learner strategies with technology. *Journal of Educational Computing Research, 22*(3), 285–322.

Ward, J. (2004). Blog assisted language learning (BALL): Push button publishing for pupils *TEFL Web Journal 3*(1). Retrieved January 23, 2007, from http://www.teflweb-j.org/v3n1/blog_ward.pdf.

Warschauer, M. (1998). *Electronic literacies: Language, culture, and power in online education.* Mahwah, NJ: Lawrence Erlbaum.

Warschauer, M., & Healey, D. (1998). Computers and language learning: An overview. *Language Teaching, 31,* 57–71.

Warschauer, M., & Kern, R. (Eds.). (2000). *Network-based language teaching: Concepts and practice.* New York: Cambridge University Press.

4

Starting the Game: CALL Activities for Your Classroom

James Aubry, Sha Balize, Zhaohui Chen,
Sabine Siekman, Iona Sarieva,
and Ruth Roux-Rodriguez

Dear Teachers,

You may feel insecure and unprepared for the journey our book is about to take you on.…No need to worry just — take a peek behind the glass of your regular classroom, and you will see some of the computer resources you have already mastered and you can easily include them in your classroom activities.

Enjoy Word Processing With Your Students

Activity 1: Reading Discussion: Describing Story Sequences and Events

- ♦ Nature of the activity: Students use Microsoft Word **AutoShapes** function to create a flowchart that describes a process or sequence of events in a story.

- ♦ Type of activity: This is a small-group activity in which students discuss a story that they have read individually prior to the activity. During the discussion, they will create a flowchart to present the events described in the story.

- ♦ Proficiency level: Advanced beginning to advanced fluency.

- ♦ Time: 10–20 minutes (individual reading time not included).

- ♦ Skills: Speaking, reading, and writing skills in the target language.

- ♦ Additional materials: Word processing software, printer.

Prior to the activity, the teacher assigns a text that presents the target culture and is written in the target language. Students read the text individually. The teacher divides the class into small groups of two to four. In each group, students decide who will enter the discussion outcomes into the Word document. The students are instructed to create a flowchart that presents the events in the story in sequence using the **AutoShapes** function in Word. After they finish creating their flowchart, the students can e-mail the charts to the teacher or print and hand them in.

Standards met in this activity...	
ACTFL Standards	**ISTE NETS Standards**
1.1, 1.2, 2.1, 5.1, 5.2	I-A, II-C, II-D, III-A, III-B, III-C

Activity 2: Reading Discussion: Presenting Main and Secondary Ideas

- ♦ Nature of the activity: Students use the **Arrow, Text Box,** and **Oval** buttons to make diagrams or mind-maps to represent main and secondary ideas in a reading.

- ♦ Type of activity: This is a small-group activity in which students discuss a story that they have read individually prior to the activity. They will create a diagram or mind-map presenting the main and secondary ideas of the story.

- ♦ Proficiency level: Advanced beginning to advanced fluency.

- ♦ Time: 10–20 minutes (individual reading time not included).

- ♦ Skills: Speaking, reading, and writing skills in the target language.

- ♦ Additional materials: Word processing software.

Prior to the activity, the teacher assigns a text in the target language that students read individually. The teacher divides the class into small groups of two to four. In each group, students decide who will enter the discussion outcomes into the Word document. The students are instructed to create a diagram or a mind-map that presents the main and secondary ideas in the story using the **Arrow, Text Box,** and **Oval** buttons. (For more technologically advanced students, it might be a good idea to encourage them to use different colors, shapes, fill effects, and lines to format their charts. The **Format AutoShape** menu is available by right-clicking on an individual shape). After students finish creating their flowchart, the teacher may ask the students to submit the charts by e-mail or print and hand them in.

Standards met in this activity...	
ACTFL Standards	**ISTE NETS Standards**
1.1, 2.1, 5.2	I-A, II-C, II-D, III-A, III-B, III-C

Activity 3: Writing With the Teacher

♦ Nature of the activity: Collaborative text planning and writing.

♦ Type of activity: This is a group activity that can be performed on one computer only. The teacher leads the activity using the computer.

♦ Proficiency level: Beginning to early intermediate fluency.

♦ Time: 15–30 minutes.

♦ Skills: Speaking, reading, and writing skills in the target language.

♦ Additional materials: Word processing software, LCD projector, printer.

During the activity, the teacher and students create a written electronic text on a topic of their choice. The teacher works on the computer, implementing the students suggestions and ideas. All of the changes are projected onto a screen so that students can follow them and participate in the text-writing process. After the LCD projector is set up and a new Word document is open, the teacher introduces the writing topic to the students and types the title. The teacher asks the students to brainstorm on the topic. During the brainstorming session, the teacher types the ideas that the students generate. The teacher and the students discuss the generated ideas. During this discussion, the teacher arranges the sentences, words, phrases by dragging and dropping them. After the ideas are organized, the teacher and students work on the beginning and the ending of their composition, making sure that a main idea and an appropriate conclusion are present. Next, the teacher and students work on the body of the text, completing sentences (if any of the ideas were given as phrases) and inserting the appropriate transitions (if applicable for their proficiency level). The teacher and students reread the text and correct any grammatical mistakes. Let students enjoy their writing product! The teacher and students can format the text together, deciding on the font size, color, position and inserting graphics and images if appropriate.

Note: The text created during this activity can be used for a variety of reading activities.

Standards met in this activity...	
ACTFL Standards	**ISTE NETS Standards**
1.1, 1.3, 5.2	I-A, II-A, III-B, III-C, IV-A, IV-D

Activity 4: Getting Ready to Write

♦ Nature of the activity: Small-group brainstorming activity.

♦ Type of activity: This is a small-group activity that requires students to work collaboratively to brainstorm ideas for a future writing assignment and create a concept map of their ideas using the **AutoShapes** function in Word.

♦ Proficiency level: Advanced beginning to advanced fluency.

- ◆ Time: 25 minutes.

- ◆ Skills: Speaking, reading, and writing skills in the target language

- ◆ Additional materials: Word processing software.

The teacher divides the class into small groups of two to four. In each group, students decide who will enter the discussion outcomes into the Word document. The theme of the composition is presented by the teacher, and students are instructed to brainstorm ideas for the assigned topic and create a concept map of these ideas. The concept map may be printed at the end of the discussion session so that students can continue working on the writing assignment individually, or it can be e-mailed to each student if the they will be using a word processing application to continue working on their writing.

Standards met in this activity...	
ACTFL Standards	ISTE NETS Standards
1.1, 1.3, 3.2, 5.2	I-A, II-A, III-B, III-C, IV-A, IV-D

Activity 5: Writing Together

- ◆ Nature of the activity: Collaborative composition outlining.

- ◆ Type of activity: This is a small-group activity that requires students to work collaboratively to put together a Word document presenting a short outline of a composition that each student will develop individually. This activity can be used as a continuation of Activity 4: Getting Ready to Write.

- ◆ Proficiency level: Advanced beginning to advanced fluency.

- ◆ Time: 20 minutes.

- ◆ Skills: Speaking, reading, and writing skills in the target language.

- ◆ Additional materials: Word processing software.

The teacher divides the class into small groups of two to four. In each group, students decide who will enter the discussion outcomes into the Word document. The theme of the composition is assigned, or, if the students have already brainstormed using Word **AutoShapes** function, the concept maps developed by the students are provided. The students are instructed to develop an outline for the composition and create a Word document presenting this outline in a bullet-point format. The outline may be printed at the end of the discussion session if students will handwrite their compositions, or it can be e-mailed to each student if they will be using a word processing application to finish their writing.

Note: For more advanced learners, ask students to search the Web for information related to the topic of the writing assignment.

Standards met in this activity...	
ACTFL Standards	**ISTE NETS Standards**
1.1, 1.3, 3.2, 5.2	I-A, II-A, III-B, III-C, IV-A, IV-D

Activity 6: Did You Find the Error?

- ◆ Nature of the activity: Collaborative work focused on form.

- ◆ Type of activity: This is a pair activity that allows students to focus on form while working with written text. The goal is to focus students on the grammar of the target language.

- ◆ Proficiency level: Advanced beginning to advanced fluency.

- ◆ Time: about 20 minutes (depending on the length of the text and the number of errors that students need to find and correct).

- ◆ Skills: Speaking, reading, and writing skills in the target language, with a focus on grammar.

- ◆ Additional materials: Word processing software and printed text.

The teacher divides the students into pairs. In each pair, student A receives an electronic version of a text that contains errors (depending on the focus of the lesson, these might be errors in spelling, agreement, tense, conjunctions, punctuation, or sequencing of ideas. Student B receives the correct version of the same text. Each pair must find the errors together without student A seeing the correct version. The comparison will be made during the process of oral interaction between the two students. After finding the errors, students should correct them in the electronic document.

Variations include the following:

- ◆ This activity could also be done without handing out the correct answers.

- ◆ Students could be encouraged to discuss why certain errors need to be corrected hey could even write short explanations for each error that they correct.

- ◆ Depending on the size and proficiency level of the class, the teacher may conduct this activity as a competition among the pairs.

Standards met in this activity...	
ACTFL Standards	**ISTE NETS Standards**
1.1. Depending on the text used additional standards can be covered, such as 2.1, 3.1, 4.1	III-D, IV-A, IV-D

Enjoy E-Mail With Your Students!

Activity 1: Student–Teacher Dialogue Journal

Keeping a dialogue journal by e-mail is very easy. Dialogue journal writing is useful in helping students become more comfortable in conversational second language use and can help students write better. Students may experience some awkwardness at first, but this will improve as the exchange progresses. You might want to use the e-mail dialogue journal only once a week to keep the workload manageable.

Assign students a question or topic to discuss in the e-mail journal. The best topic is one that is connected to your other class activities. For example, students who are learning about the weather in their French class could be asked to e-mail you a few sentences about the weather in Paris or about their favorite season. Other students might be prompted to write at greater length using a particular language function or grammatical feature that has been taught. For more mature and fluent students, prompt them to examine their language learning that week, evaluating their strengths and weaknesses.

In assessing this activity, be sure to consider your objectives. Create a checklist or rubric that includes all of these objectives. If, for example, you want students to write at length, with perfect spelling, using new vocabulary, include these factors in your grading plan.

For best results, let students know the grading plan in advance. Then report the evaluation results to students to help them improve. Use the results to identify students instructional needs.

Standards met in this activity...	
ACTFL Standards	**ISTE NETS Standards**
1.1, 1.2, 1.3, 2.1, 2.2, 3.1, 3.2, 4.1, 4.2, 5.1, 5.2	I-A, I-B, II-A, II-B, II-C, II-D, II-E, III-A, III-B, III-C, III-D, IV-A, IV-B, IV-C, V-A, V-B, VI-A, VI-B, VI-C, VI-D, VI-E

Activity 2: Reflective Journal by E-Mail

Journaling works well for getting students to write you, but it's also great for you to write yourself! Use e-mail to help yourself learn the technology. Doing this will help you grow more comfortable using e-mail while developing a reflective awareness and improving your teaching.

For example, you might write yourself a note at the end of each day. You could write about your daily technology teaching experiences. Jot down, for example, your thoughts on questions such as these: What went well in class using technology? Why? What could have been improved? How? What surprised me? Is my grading plan effective? Does it include technology and language learning? Do I have confidence in the assessment results? Are the students learning more? Learning better?

In the future, when you read your journal e-mails, you might be surprised by how much you have grown. You can use this private e-mail journal to teach your colleagues how to use e-mail effectively, whether in a one-on-one setting or perhaps by giving a brief workshop in your school.

Standards met in this activity...	
ACTFL Standards	ISTE NETS Standards
1.1, 1.2, 1.3, 2.1, 2.2, 3.1, 3.2, 4.1, 4.2, 5.1, 5.2	I-A, I-B, II-A, II-B, II-C, II-D, II-E, III-A, III-B, III-C, III-D, IV-A, IV-B, IV-C, V-A, V-B, VI-A, VI-B, VI-C, VI-D, VI-E

Activity 3: Word-of-the-Day Newsletter

Challenge your students and go beyond the curriculum! You can do this by subscribing to a word-of-the-day newsletter by e-mail. These are offered in many different languages. Here are some word-a-day newsletters for many different languages:

♦ http://travlang.com/wordofday/

♦ http://www.transparent.com/wotd/index.htm

An electronic newsletter differs from an e-mail message in that it is a one-way communication in which a message is delivered to you on the set schedule, but you can't write back.

Subscribing to a word-of-the-day service introduces your students to new vocabulary. Receiving second language vocabulary tidbits by e-mail can be interesting for students. However, the learning potential is limited if students only read passively. Make the word-of-the-day service more meaningful by requiring students to do something with the new word. For example, have students use the new word in a sentence or come up with a list of synonyms or antonyms. They can identify whether the word is formal or informal and who would use it. Continue to build technology prowess, make sure the new word discussion takes place by e-mail. You can vary the grouping, asking all students to respond to you, a small group, or pairs.

Be sure to build an assessment that includes all of the important factors in your activity. Include technology skill, for example, when you have taught a technology skill, just as you would include word knowledge and spelling when you have taught vocabulary. It is especially appropriate to use e-mail in your assessment when you have been teaching by e-mail. Use assessment results to identify students strengths and weaknesses. Such information will help you plan future lessons to build on this foundation.

Standards met in this activity...	
ACTFL Standards	**ISTE NETS Standards**
1.1, 1.2, 1.3, 2.1, 2.2, 3.1, 3.2, 4.1, 4.2, 5.1, 5.2	I-A, I-B, II-A, II-B, II-C, II-D, II-E, III-A, III-B, III-C, III-D, IV-A, IV-B, IV-C, V-A, V-B, VI-A, VI-B, VI-C, VI-D, VI-E

Activity 4: Electronic Postcard Exchange

Want a new twist on foreign language writing? Have your students exchange electronic postcards by e-mail! Writing can be even more creative with e-cards. Try out the paired writing activity to see how.

The steps vary on different sites, so check out the sites you plan to use. Practice in advance by sending e-cards to yourself or to family or friends.

To use e-cards with your language students, first assign a student to write to another learner. Alternatively, you could assign a pair to write to another pair. You could also jumble the senders and recipients, so that Student A writes to Student B, and Student B writes to Student C. You can add some interest by including a mystery writer in this activity: Do not announce all of the writer–recipient pairs to the whole class. In other words, tell Student X to write to Student Y, but don't tell Student X who will write to him or her. The recipient must guess the writer's identity.

Give writers the Yahoo! Mail addresses of their assigned recipients. Visit an e-card site from those listed here. For variety, assign different students to different sites. (This will also help prevent slow Internet traffic on the sites.)

Have students plan their message, keeping it secret from the recipient. Challenge your students to use recently taught structures or vocabulary words. They might also describe the e-card image in the postcard message, or they might write a poem or joke based on the e-card image. If you are keeping the classmate's identity secret, the mystery writer can drop hints as to his or her identity.

Have students type their e-card messages to their assigned classmates, filling in the form on the Web site. Clicking the **Submit** or **Send** button usually sends the e-card.

Direct students to go to the Yahoo! Mail site, log in, and check their inboxes. The e-mail message will notify the recipient to go to a particular Web address. Students can simply click on this Web link, automatically jumping to the page with the e-card from the classmate. (This page is usually active for 30 days.)

After students have read the e-card they received, they can write about it. They can describe, using the target language, the steps they took to complete this activity; they can discuss the experience of writing and reading in the target language through e-cards; they can evaluate their performance; and they can discuss what they learned through this experience.

In addition, recipients can guess the writer's identity, if you have used the mystery writer variation. Tell students to submit these written reflections to you by e-mail.

Use students' e-mail reflections as one factor in evaluating learning. Construct a checklist or rubric for this activity, being sure to include all of the factors that are crucial to your lesson objectives. Some teachers may focus on target cultural knowledge, for example, whereas others may emphasize target language fluency. Consider whether you expect students to analyze, summarize, or evaluate. If so, include these factors on your checklist. Measure all of the key skills and information from the activity: If it is important, measure it!

The following Web sites offer free e-cards:

- http://www.takingitglobal.org/express/ecards/ (to search for images related to a particular country, click Global Gallery E-Cards in the sidebar)

- http://yahooligans.yahoo.com/content/ecards/ (safe, child-friendly environment; English language)

- http://www.toonscanada.com/ (e-cards only in an English-language, child-friendly environment)

- http://www.cyber-cards.com (e-cards and virtual gifts)

- http://www.regards.com/ (nice variety of cards)

- http://mail.yahoo.com (convenient access from Yahoo! Mail site)

Standards met in this activity...	
ACTFL Standards	**ISTE NETS Standards**
1.1, 1.2, 1.3, 2.1, 2.2, 3.1, 3.2, 4.1, 4.2, 5.1, 5.2	I-A, I-B, II-A, II-B, II-C, II-D, II-E, III-A, III-B, III-C, III-D, IV-A, IV-B, IV-C, V-A, V-B, VI-A, VI-B, VI-C, VI-D, VI-E

Activity 5: E-Mail Chain Story

A chain story is a simple activity that can be used to develop creativity or reinforce grammar lessons. Stories are written by multiple authors; each writer contributes a sentence to the story, then forwards the entire text to a partner. Each story will be unique. Chain stories work especially well at intermediate or higher proficiency levels, but even beginners can craft a simple story.

Before class, prepare a list of student groups. Divide students into small groups ideally, groups of three. Include group member names and Yahoo! Mail addresses on each list. (This guide is structured with a triad in mind. Modify the activity if you need different groupings, but large groups may not be able to finish the stories.)

Before class, write the first line for several different chain stories. You will need three different story starters if you have three members in a group. (For larger groups, you will need to write more story beginnings.) Create stories to work with topics, structures, functions, or genres you have covered recently, so that students can build on this foundation. Try to make the starter interesting or intriguing. Examples include the following:

- When I was going to class a dog came up to me and he started talking to me.

- It was a dark and stormy night...

- I went out to eat last night, and you won't believe what I had for dinner.

- I used to laugh at stories about monsters, but now I'm not so sure. Let me tell you why.

- It was a sunny day in Paris when I saw the surprise of my life.

- Let me tell you about the year 2020...

Before class, e-mail the chain story starters to the students. Each triad member will receive a different story starter. For example, Student A in every group might receive "When I was going to class a dog came up to me and he started talking to me." Send the second triad member a different story starter, perhaps "Let me tell you about the year 2020...." Then e-mail the last member of every group a different story beginning, such as "It was a dark and stormy night...."

In class, you explain to students that they will work in groups of three, adding to and completing three different stories. Hand out triad assignments and student Yahoo! Mail addresses. Each student will log in to his or her Yahoo! Mail account to access the story beginning e-mail that you have sent. To that sentence, the learner will add a second sentence. This student will forward the two-line story to another group member. At the same time, this student will receive a different two-line story from another group member. The student must write a third line. The e-mail chain story can continue as long as you wish.

Have student groups judge which story best represents the group's work, whether it is the best story, the strangest, or the funniest. They must choose the story and explain why they selected it. They will forward this story, and the rationale for their choice, to you.

Structure your assessment according to what you have taught and how you have taught it. This activity might address particular topics, structures, functions, or genres. You might use this activity so that students write at length, or you might set a time limit and require students to write rapidly. You will be using technology and sharing writing, so these are elements that should come into assessment. Students are developing their judgment of quality and their writing skills (because they are required to evaluate their stories and select one, justifying this choice). These factors should also be assessed in your performance evaluation. Quality assessment is time-consuming, but the results are worth it. You will have a solid basis for making educational decisions about your students.

Standards met in this activity...	
ACTFL Standards	**ISTE NETS Standards**
1.1, 1.2, 1.3, 2.1, 2.2, 3.1, 3.2, 4.1, 4.2, 5.1, 5.2	I-A, I-B, II-A, II-B, II-C, II-D, II-E, III-A, III-B, III-C, III-D, IV-A, IV-B, IV-C, V-A, V-B, VI-A, VI-B, VI-C, VI-D, VI-E

Enjoy Yahoo! GeoCities Web Site Builder With Your Students

Activity 1: Part I: Searching for Information

- ◆ Nature of the activity: Collaborative work.

- ◆ Type of activity: This is a group activity that encourages collaboration among students as they search for relevant information in the target language. The goal is to engage students in using the target language and browsing Web sites written in the target language.

- ◆ Proficiency level: Intermediate to advanced fluency.

- ◆ Time: The activity can be modified to suit different time frames, for example, a 50-minute class that asks students to form groups and search for information on different topics. It can also be conducted as an after-class collaboration among students in small groups.

- ◆ Skills: Speaking and reading in the target language, with a focus on communication. This activity involves higher-order thinking skills, such as selecting, organizing, and synthesizing information.

The teacher divides students into small groups of three or four. Each group is assigned a different topic, for example, a cultural aspect of the target language. Students in each group work together at a learning center with computers and Internet access to search for information about their topic in the target language. Each group should discuss (in the target language) what they found and compile a list of annotated resources.

Standards met in this activity...	
ACTFL Standards	**ISTE NETS Standards**
1.1, 1.3, 3.2, 5.1	I-A, I-D, II-B, II-D

Activity 1: Part II: Building a Group Resource Web Site

♦ Nature of the activity: Collaborative work.

♦ Type of activity: This is a group activity that requires students to work in small groups to share resources that they locate online.

♦ Proficiency level: Intermediate to advanced fluency.

♦ Time: This activity can be done in stages depending on the work process of the groups.

♦ Skills: Speaking, reading, and writing skills in the target language.

After completing Part I, have each group register for a Yahoo! GeoCities Web space and build a Web site using the resources they found online.

Standards met in this activity...	
ACTFL Standards	ISTE NETS Standards
1.1, 1.3, 3.2, 5.1	I-A, I-D, II-B, II-D

Activity 2: Web Site Swap

♦ Nature of the activity: Collaborative work.

♦ Type of activity: This activity allows groups of students to share their Web sites and to learn about and critique other groups Web sites.

♦ Proficiency level: Intermediate to advanced fluency.

♦ Time: About 50 minutes, depending on the discussion within and among groups.

♦ Skills: Speaking and reading skills in the target language, with a focus on communication.

After completing Activity 1, have groups swap their Web sites in the class. Each group will browse the Web site assigned to them and learn and critique the content, design, etc. The whole class will have a discussion about the Web sites. All of the verbal communication should be in the target language.

Standards met in this activity...	
ACTFL Standards	ISTE NETS Standards
1.1, 1.3, 3.2, 5.1	I-A, I-D, II-B, II-D

Activity 3: My Own Space

- ◆ Nature of the activity: Individual work.

- ◆ Type of activity: This activity allows students to work on their individual Web sites. Topics can be self-chosen, or options can be given by the teacher. The Web site should be written in the target language.

- ◆ Proficiency level: Intermediate to advanced fluency.

- ◆ Time: Variable.

- ◆ Skills: Reading and writing skills in the target language.

The class begins by discussing topics for personal Web sites. Each student should choose a topic or comes up with his or her own topic. Have each student register for a Yahoo! Geocities Web site and then research and build his or her own Web site.

Standards met in this activity...	
ACTFL Standards	ISTE NETS Standards
1.1, 1.3, 3.2, 5.1	I-A, I-D, II-B, II-D

Activity 4: The Textbook Online — Revision Work

- ◆ Nature of the activity: Group work.

- ◆ Type of activity: This activity requires students to review work from the textbook they are using in class. Often, it is a good idea for students to create a project based on the work they have been doing in class. By carrying out this work, it simultaneously acts as revision. In this activity, groups of students create Web sites on which they revise work they have already done in class. The Web site should be written in the target language.

- ◆ Proficiency level: Beginner to advanced fluency.

- ◆ Time: Variable.

- ◆ Skills: Reading and writing skills in the target language, as well as revision.

Have the groups discuss topics that could be the subject of their revision. Each group constructs revision exercises (vocabulary, grammar, culture, content) that are placed on their Web sites. Students may want to go to http://www.quia.com or http://hotpot.uvic.ca/, sites that enable users to create interactive multiple-choice, short-answer, jumbled-sentence, crossword, matching/ordering, and fill-in-the blank exercises. When finished, each group asks another group go to their site and do the revision exercises.

Standards met in this activity...	
ACTFL Standards	ISTE NETS Standards
1.1, 1.3, 3.2, 5.1	I-A, I-D, II-B, II-D

Activity 5: Creating a Big Book

- ◆ Nature of the activity: Individual or group work.

- ◆ Type of activity: Have you ever seen an interactive big book used in elementary school classes? The students are riveted to the book! The teacher reads the story, and when the teacher comes to the end of the page, listeners have a choice as to how the plot will progress. For example, if they want the story to head in direction A, they turn to page 16, but if they want the plot to go in direction B, they turn to page 10. This provides the teacher with opportunities to discuss and introduce new concepts, depending on the theme of the book. In this activity, students create their own online big books focused on a chapter of the textbook they are using.

- ◆ Proficiency level: Beginner to advanced fluency.

- ◆ Time: Variable.

- ◆ Skills: Reading and writing skills in the target language, as well as revision.

Have groups choose a topic that will be the focus of the big book. Each group constructs a story board (plot line) on paper. Once the story board is created, students can start creating the necessary Web pages and links. When finished, each group reads their story to the class (presentation can use an LCD projector).

Standards met in this activity...	
ACTFL Standards	ISTE NETS Standards
1.1, 1.3, 3.2, 5.1	I-A, I-D, II-B, II-D

Search Engines in Languages Other Than English

German

http://www.searchenginecolossus.com/Germany.html (collection of German search engines)

http://abacho.com/

http://de.altavista.com/

http://www.google.de/

French

http://www.searchenginecolossus.com/France.html (collection of French search engines)

http://www.google.fr/

http://www.francite.com/

http://infoseek.go.com/

http://www.nathan.de/

http://www.sharelook.de/

http://web.de/

http://dino-online.de/

http://www-fr.lycos.com/

http://abondance.com/

http://nomade.tiscali.fr/

http://wanadoo.fr/

Spanish

http://www.searchenginecolossus.com/ Spain.html (collection of Spanish search engines)

http://www.searchenginecolossus.com/ Mexico.html (collection of Mexican search engines)

http://es.altavista.com/

http://www.google.com/intl/es/

Russian

http://www.searchenginecolossus.com/ Russia.html (collection of Russian search engines)

http://www.zhurnal.ru/search/engines.shtml (another collection of Russian search engines)

http://www.google.com/intl/ru/

http://www.rambler.ru/

You can find search engines for the target language that you are interested in; it is easy with Search Engine Colossus! Type **http://www.searchenginecolossus.com/name of the country.html**, for example, **http://www.searchenginecolossus.com/ Mexico.html**, and enjoy the rich collection of search engines in English (about the target country) and in the target language.

Section II

E-Creation

5

Presentation Software: Language Learning and Fun with PowerPoint

Robert Summers and Ray Madrigal

I worked for hours to create a review using PowerPoint for the midterm exam for students. We scheduled it on a special day in a classroom I had never taught in before. With no curtains or shades to darken the room, the sun was as bright as in a solarium. Students struggled to see the image on the screen. With a few clicks, I was able to change the slide background and the font color of the presentation adding more contrast and making it easier to read the text. I also uploaded the PowerPoint onto my Web site so that students could view it on their own afterward.

High school French teacher

PowerPoint in the Foreign Language Classroom

At first I had only seen Microsoft PowerPoint used as a tool for giving presentations. When I attended professional meetings, the presenter would use it instead of a whiteboard or overhead transparencies. The first couple of times, I was impressed by the flashy background and moving text. However, those effects quickly became tiresome. After some initial training, I realized just how powerful and underutilized PowerPoint is. It is much more than just a way to present information to a group. I created an interactive PowerPoint to use in my classroom. It presents students with a scenario: They are planning the menu for a party. There are different types of dishes that they can choose to prepare and different stores that they visit to buy what they need. It has been so well received by my students. In fact, several of my colleagues have asked me to help them with their own PowerPoint projects.

The use of PowerPoint in the classroom supports reading, writing, speaking, and listening skills. Reading skills are augmented by the presentation of text on the screen. Students may be asked to follow directions and interactively follow hyperlinks embedded in the presentation. Writing skills are developed when students are asked to create their own presentations. These presentations should be written in the target language and reflect students' own interests. To develop students' speaking skills, audio files can be easily embedded into PowerPoint presentations, in much the same way that a user can create links to other slides or to Web sites. For example, learners can narrate a story that they have created and show it as a PowerPoint presentation. Students can ameliorate their listening skills by listening to oral texts that have been recorded and placed within a presentation. These types of materials can be created by either students or teachers. Moreover, these presentations can be used with the whole class or within learning centers for individual students working at their own pace.

A second and equally important rationale for the integration of this software program is that it is a tool that is readily available to most educators today. Microsoft Office, including Word and PowerPoint, are often preinstalled in most PCs purchased by educational institutions. If it is not installed on your own computer, most software is available for purchase at discounted rates for both students and teachers. Moreover, many teachers have become familiar with this presentation software by attending in-service meetings and other professional events. This chapter will present some very practical ideas about how to integrate PowerPoint into the foreign language classroom.

Just try this!

PowerPoint offers foreign language teachers a wonderful and creative tool for introducing language structures such as vocabulary, grammar, and culture. Slide presentations can easily be augmented with clip art or photos to pique students' interest or to illustrate a specific point. Many clip art images and photos come with the recent editions of this software package, and others can easily be downloaded from the Internet. Be sure to follow proper copyright protocols in using materials that are available online. A good rule of thumb is that most images can be used freely in an educational setting, but be sure to give credit where credit is due.

To learn the main functions of PowerPoint, you are going to learn by doing. Follow this example, in which you will create a presentation that outlines a visit to a zoo.

Step 1   Creating a new presentation

♦ After opening PowerPoint, go to **File** on the menu bar and select **New Presentation**.

Step 2 — Adding text to a title page

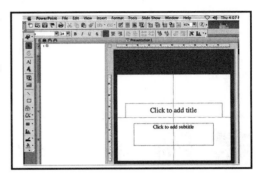

- You will then see the following screen. This is where you will make your first slide.

- Place the cursor in the box labeled **Click to add title** and type your text.

Step 3 — Inserting a picture from clip art

- After adding your title, you might want to add a picture. To do this, place your cursor in the spot where you want the picture to appear and click **Insert > Picture > Clip Art** .

Step 4 — Selecting a clip art image

- A new screen will appear. Search for the picture that you want to add. Once you have chosen a picture, select that picture, and it will be inserted where you placed your cursor.

Step 5 — Resizing and moving an image

- If you want to resize an image, click on that image to select it. You will know it is selected because squares will appear around its perimeter. Click on and hold one of the squares and drag to enlarge the picture. To move the image, click on the image, hold, and drag it to the desired location.

Step 6 — Applying a slide design

- Now that your image is appropriately sized and placed, let's add a background to your presentation. First, click on the **Slide Design** button near the top of the screen. If you are not sure what a particular button does, hover the cursor over it, and a description will appear.

♦ Note: If you can't find the **Slide Design** button, you can access this option from the **Format** menu on the menu bar.

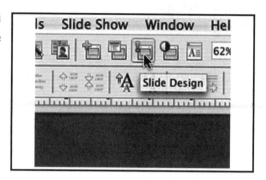

Step 7   Choosing a slide design

♦ After clicking on **Slide Design**, a new window will appear. In this window, you can select a design template for your presentation. Notice that you can choose to apply this template to all slides or just to the current slide.

Step 8   Inserting a new slide

♦ Now let's create the next slide. To do this, click on **Insert** on the menu bar at the top of your screen and choose **New Slide**.

Step 9   Changing the slide layout

♦ The new slide will appear, using the same layout and background as the previous slide. Let's change the slide layout to show both text and a picture.

♦ First, click on the **Slide Layout** button near the top of the screen. It is located to the right of the **Slide Design** button. Remember, if you are not sure what a particular a button does, hover the cursor over it and a description will appear.

♦ Note: If you can't find the **Slide Layout** button, you can access this option from the **Format** menu on the menu bar.

Step 10   Choosing a slide layout

♦ After clicking **Slide Layout**, a new window will appear. Here, you can choose how you would like your slide to be arranged.

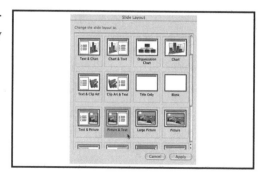

Step 11　Adding a picture to the slide layout

◆ After applying the new layout to your slide, add your text. Double click on the **Double click to add picture** icon to add a picture.

Step 12　Inserting a picture from a file

◆ A new window will appear. Browse to the file that you want to insert and select it. Depending on its size, you may need to resize the picture (Step 5).

Step 13　Adding slide transitions

◆ Next, let's add a transition from the first slide to the second slide. First, select **Slide Show** on the menu bar. Next, select **Slide Transition**.

Step 14　Choosing a slide transition

◆ A new screen will appear. On this screen, you can adjust the type of transition and its speed, and you can include a sound that either is provided in PowerPoint or that you have created yourself. Notice that the window to the left of the drop-down menu provides a preview of your transition.

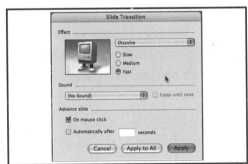

◆ At the very bottom of this screen, you can choose when to advance the screen (in seconds). The default is set to **On mouse click**, but you can switch to automatic timing. This is particularly useful if you are creating a presentation that will play at a stand-alone kiosk.

Step 15　Adding animation

◆ Let's move on and create another slide. On this slide, I have already inserted text and a picture. Let's animate the picture. To do this, select the picture and then, on the menu bar, select **Slide Show** and then **Animation**. When you scroll over **Animation**, a submenu will appear. There are several default animations that you can choose from. Experiment to find the one that you like best.

◆ You can also animate text in the same way that you animate a picture. For more complex animations, choose **Custom** on the animation submenu.

Step 16 Creating links within a presentation

◆ Within a presentation, you can create hyperlinks that take the user to a Web site, saved file (such as a Word document or spreadsheet), another page in your PowerPoint presentation, or e-mail address.

◆ Let's add a link to this presentation. First, highlight the text or image to which you'd like to add a hyperlink. On the menu bar, select **Insert > Hyperlink**.

Step 17 Choosing a link type and target

◆ A new window will appear. In this window, type in the Web address to which you wish to link. You can also link to another document or to an e-mail address.

Step 18 Adding a text box

◆ Sometimes, you might want to add text on top of a picture or elsewhere on a slide. This can be done using a text box. On the **Drawing** toolbar, click on the **Text Box** button.

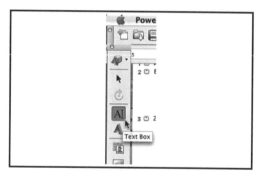

Step 19 Sizing a text box

◆ Drag the cursor over the area where you would like the text to appear. Don't worry if it is too small or too large. You can resize the text box and change the font size and color after you enter your text.

◆ The text box will disappear when you click another button. If this happens, just click on the area where you originally placed the text box, and it will reappear.

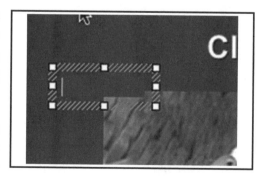

Step 20   Formatting a text box

♦ After entering your text, you may want to change the background color of the text box or the border. To do this, first select the text box. When it is selected, white squares will appear around the text box. Next, go to the **Format** menu on the menu bar and select **Text Box**.

Step 21   Changing colors and lines

♦ A new window will appear. Here, you can change the fill color, line color, and transparency of the text box.

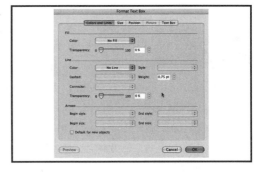

Step 22   Adding arrows

♦ Now that you have added the text boxes, changed their backgrounds, and added a borer, let's draw arrows to the fish so that everyone will know their names.

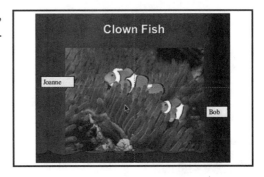

Step 23   Creating AutoShapes

♦ To draw arrows, select the **AutoShapes** button from the drawing toolbar. A submenu will appear.

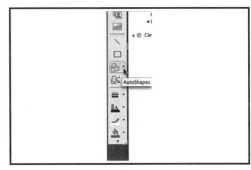

Step 24 Choosing AutoShapes

♦ On the submenu, choose the shape that you want to use. There are many different AutoShapes from which to choose. Don't just limit to arrows—explore and see what different other shapes you might add.

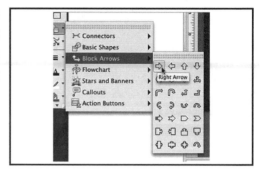

Step 25 Drawing an AutoShape

♦ Your cursor will change to a crosshair. Drag and hold the cursor until the arrow is the desired size. By selecting an AutoShape and clicking on **Format** on the menu bar, you can change background color and the outline of your AutoShape, just as we did with the text box.

Now you are getting it!

Step 26 Adding WordArt

♦ Now let's add a new slide with an exciting title. To make this title, we will use **WordArt**. First, place your cursor on the spot where you want the WordArt to appear. Next, select **Insert WordArt** on the drawing toolbar.

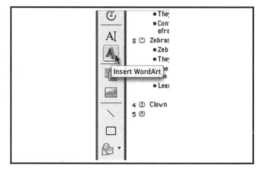

Step 27 Choosing a WordArt style

♦ A new screen will appear. Here, you can select the type of WordArt that you want insert.

Step 28 Entering WordArt text

♦ A new screen will appear. Here, you can type your text and can change the font and size of the text.

Step 29 Resizing and positioning WordArt

♦ Click **OK**, and your text will appear as WordArt. You can change the size and position of the WordArt as you would an image or clip art.

Step 30 Adding narration

♦ In the foreign language classroom, audio can be an invaluable tool. Now, let's add audio narration to our slide. Select **Slide Show** from the menu bar, and then click on **Record Narration**. The slide will fill the whole screen, and the computer will begin recording. No indication of the recording will be given except that the slide will appear in the full screen. When you have finished recording, press **Escape**.

Step 31 Checking your recording

♦ After you have finished recording, you will see a small speaker icon in the lower right-hand corner of the screen. Click on this icon to listen to your narration.

Step 32 Adding action buttons

♦ Action buttons allow users to navigate through a PowerPoint presentation. To add an action button, follow the procedure for creating an AutoShape (Step 23), but this time, select **Action Button** from the **AutoShape** submenu.

Step 33 — Selecting an action button

◆ On the **Action Button** submenu, there are 12 buttons to choose from. These buttons are useful if you want to use a presentation at a stand-alone kiosk.

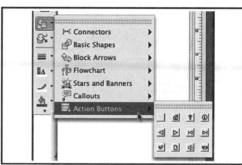

◆ The buttons are intuitively labeled. For example, the ◁ button, when pressed, takes you to the previous slide.

◆ Once you have chosen the action button that you want to use, your cursor will become a crosshair. Click and hold the mouse to draw the action button that you have chosen.

You have got something to smile about!

Step 34 — Formatting action buttons

◆ When you release the mouse button after drawing the action button in, a new menu will appear. On this menu, you can create action settings, such as linking the button to slides, sounds, or files. You can also decide whether you want the action button to become active on a click or a mouse-over.

◆ The default setting for the ◁ button is a hyperlink to the previous slide on mouse click. You can change these settings if you want to link to a different slide or even play a sound.

Step 35 — Making a **Click to hear** button

◆ After you have created a sound in another program or imported one from a CD, you can insert the sound using an action button. The sound will play when the action button is pressed.

♦ Insert an action button as you did in Steps 32–34. When the **Action Button** submenu appears, check the box that says **Play Sound** and select a sound from the drop-down menu.

♦ In this example, we are inserting a sound file that we made; therefore, we would select **Other Sound**. However, you could also select a sound that is already included in PowerPoint.

Step 36   Browsing for a sound file

♦ After you have selected **Other Sound** from the drop-down menu, a new window will appear. In this window, you can search for the sound file that you created.

♦ Once you have selected your sound file, click **Insert**.

Step 37   Confirming the sound file selection

♦ After clicking **Insert**, a new menu will appear. On this menu, you can confirm that you have selected the appropriate file and that it will play either on mouse click or mouse-over.

♦ Press **OK**, and the sound will play when you click on the action button that you have created.

Step 38   Formatting action buttons

♦ You might want to change the color or the outline style of an action button. To do so, select the button by clicking on it. You will know it is selected when six small, white squares appear around the box's perimeter. Next, select **Format > AutoShape**.

Step 39   Changing AutoShape color and style

♦ After selecting **AutoShape** on the **Format** menu, you will see the following screen.

♦ On this menu, you can change the color, outline color, or transparency of the AutoShape. After selecting the style of the button you want, click **OK**.

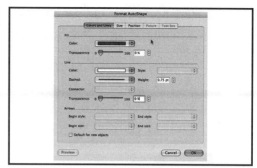

Step 40 Adding text to an AutoShape

♦ Now that the action button plays a sound when it is clicked, it may not be clear to everyone that sees the presentation. Let's add text to the shape so that the function of the button will be obvious.

♦ On the **Drawing** toolbar, select **Text Box**. Your cursor will change. Next, click and hold the mouse button and draw the area where you want to type your text.

♦ Type your text and click out of the box.

Step 41 Changing text font and color in a text box

♦ You may need to change the text color or style in order for the text to be legible. To do so, select the text box, highlight the text inside the box, and then change the font and color using the **Formatting** toolbar. The adjusted text will be shown in the following image.

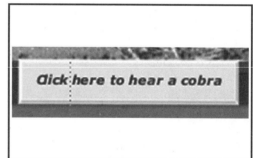

♦ If the **Formatting** toolbar is not visible, go to **View > Toolbars** make sure that **Formatting** is checked. This works for all toolbars.

♦ On a PC, the easiest way to use international characters in PowerPoint is to create them in a word processing program and then copy and paste them into your presentation. On a Mac, the same shortcuts you use to create international characters in word processing programs work in PowerPoint.

Tricks and Traps

♦ **Trap:** Be careful when inserting photographs obtained from image search engines on the Internet. Copyright laws need to be kept in mind. For amateur photographers, this is an opportunity to be creative with your own photos.

• **Trick:** Fortunately, there are many appropriate images, clip art images, and photos available for free on the Internet. Just be sure to give proper credit. Model this behavior for your students, and they will get the idea, too.

♦ **Trap:** Sometimes it is difficult to foresee how an image or photo will appear on a classroom screen or how special effects will appear in the classroom.

• **Trick:** Plan on pre-testing your presentation under classroom conditions. Only then will you be able to determine what your presentation will look like—consider factors such as sunlight reflections, fluorescent lighting, or even a damaged screen. Pre-testing is like a dress rehearsal for a dramatic production. It gives you an opportunity to work out the kinks in your slide presentation.

♦ **Trap:** If you are planning on having students design their own presentations, be sure to stress that their work should be content driven. Often, students get caught up in the technology and focus more on making a flashy presentation.

• **Trick:** Create a specific rubric that places importance on the content and language that students use. Technology is only a container for students' language use.

Reflections

♦ What units or modules in your current textbook would benefit from a supplemental PowerPoint presentation?

♦ How could your students get involved in creating, developing, or adapting PowerPoint presentations in their language learning?

♦ Keep a journal of your PowerPoint presentation experiments. List the names of your slide shows and how you used them, and reflect on the positive benefits of your slide show, ways that you improve or change it, and any technical glitches that you dealt with.

Name of Slide Show	How I Used It	Benefits of Using It	Ways to Improve	Technical Glitches
My first slide show	Told a story about my trip to Paris to my class	Visuals and text helped comprehension	Use few sounds effects and enhance with my interesting transitions	Sound didn't work, realized that I need to connect speakers to my laptop
My second slide show	Taught verbs of motion	....	....	....

Enjoy!

Here are several activities to get you started.

Activity 1: E-Flash Cards

♦ Nature of the activity: Vocabulary review.

♦ Type of activity: Individual or paired group activity.

♦ Proficiency level: All levels.

♦ Time: Allow 20 to 30 minutes for students to create a slide presentation.

♦ Skills: Reading and speaking skills of thematic vocabulary

♦ Additional materials: Current text or syllabus materials; current vocabulary.

The teacher divides the students into pairs. Students can be paired strategically, so that both are at similar or different levels of language learning. The students work collaboratively to create a slide presentation to practice, review, and drill targeted vocabulary from the current theme in the syllabus (e.g., the study of food items and the food pyramid). The students create a slide presentation with an assigned number of vocabulary items, say, 10 or 20. They can insert images or photos of different food items, including markets where such items are bought or restaurants where such dishes are served. Depending on the time available and the students' level of technical ability, students can be assigned to "spice up" their presentations by recording their voices as they pronounce the words or phrases used in their slide presentation.

Standards met in this activity...	
ACTFL Standards	**ISTE NETS Standards**
1.2, 1.3, 2.2	I-B, II-A, II-B, III-A, III-B, III-C, III-D

Activity 2: The Classroom

♦ Nature of the activity: Vocabulary.

♦ Type of activity: Paired group activity.

♦ Proficiency level: Beginners.

♦ Time: Allow 30 minutes for students to take pictures and 20 minutes to create a slide presentation.

♦ Skills: Speaking skills of thematic vocabulary.

♦ Additional materials: Current text or syllabus materials; current vocabulary.

Have students work in pairs. The task is to take several digital photos of items found in any classroom. Of course, this activity works if students are already are familiar with the vocabulary words for classroom items in the target language.

Have students take pictures of items such as books, backpacks, pencils, blackboards, overhead projectors, and calculators and then download the photos to PCs. Have students create a PowerPoint slide show of their classroom items by going to the **Design Template**. The **Auto Content Wizard** will help them insert their photos to create a slide presentation. Have students share their photos with their classmates. As they present their photo albums, their classmates can respond orally by calling out the appropriate words or phrases in the target language.

A variation of this activity would be to have each group of students "specialize" in one theme, such as the classroom, the library, or the gymnasium. Or students could use this activity as a general review for several thematic units, with each group of students creating and presenting a slide show on that theme.

Standards met in this activity...	
ACTFL Standards	**ISTE NETS Standards**
1.2, 1.3, 2.2, 5.1	II-A, III-A, III-B, III-D, V-C, VI-C, VI-E

Activity 3: Jeopardy!

♦ Nature of the activity: The teacher uses PowerPoint to create a Jeopardy! game.

♦ Type of activity: Group activity.

- Proficiency level: All levels.

- Time: 30–40 minutes (depending on the number of questions).

- Skills: Reading and speaking skills in the target language.

- Additional material: Current text or syllabus materials; current vocabulary.

PowerPoint can easily be used to create a Jeopardy! game. There are several Web sites available that provide ready-made Jeopardy PowerPoint templates, along with step-by-step instructions for adapting this popular game to your content. For example, check out http://www.graves.k12.ky.us/tech/jeopardy_instructions.htm.

Download this template and save it to your computer. Open the file and save it for the unit content that you wish to cover in the activity. Fill in the appropriate categories with the content and arrange them according to level of difficulty. More points should be awarded for more difficult vocabulary, cultural, or grammatical items.

Plan how you will group your students for the execution of this activity. Small groups seem to work best. Remember to pre-test your Jeopardy! game in class-like conditions.

Students love activities that consist of games or competitions. Be prepared to offer some type of reward or special privilege to the winners of the game. Have fun using PowerPoint presentation software to productively review your language content in a fun and interesting way!

Standards met in this activity…	
ACTFL Standards	**ISTE NETS Standards**
1.1, 1.2, 1.3, 2.1, 2.2, 3.2	II-B, III-A, III-B, III-C, III-D, V-D, VI-D

Activity 4: Language Portfolio

- Nature of the activity: Review presentation.

- Type of activity: Individual activity.

- Proficiency level: All levels.

- Time: Ongoing.

- Skills: Reading, writing, listening, and speaking skills of thematic vocabulary.

- Additional materials: Current text or syllabus materials; current vocabulary; previous projects completed in class.

Toward the end of the school year, have students create a slide show that summarizes their previous activities. These activities don't have to be electronically based—they could be scanned and saved electronically. Ask students to start with an introductory slide that tells a little bit about themselves. They might also list the assignments in the introductory slide and link the titles to the materials. After each student has created his or her own portfolio, create a class portfolio that showcases the work of all of your students. Remember that portfolios should show more than just the best work of students; instead, they should detail a student's growth, illustrated by classroom artifacts.

Standards met in this activity...	
ACTFL Standards	ISTE NETS Standards
1.2, 1.3, 2.1, 2.2, 4.1, 5.1	II-A, III-A, III-B, III-D, V-C, VI-C, VI-E

Activity 5: Culture

♦ Nature of the activity: Vocabulary review.

♦ Type of activity: Individual or paired group activity.

♦ Proficiency level: All levels.

♦ Time: Allow 20–30 minutes for students to create a slide presentation.

♦ Skills: Reading and speaking skills of thematic vocabulary

♦ Additional materials: Current text or syllabus materials; current vocabulary.

Have students (individually or in groups) download images, artwork, or photos from a specific country in which the target language is spoken. You can create a WebQuest to narrow and focus their search (see Chapter 13 in this book). German students, for example, may wish to focus on characters such as Hansel and Gretel. Spanish students focusing on Mexican culture may create slides on Aztec civilization, including the architectural monuments of the pyramids of Teotihuacan. Many such photos can easily be found on the Internet. See, for example, the following Web site for archeological information about the famous City of the Gods of the Aztec civilization: http://archaeology.la.asu.edu/teo/.

Ask students to create and edit a PowerPoint presentation that demonstrates what they learned from their WebQuest research on the culture of the target language. Have students share their work with each other. This can be done by providing class time for individual or group presentations or even by having students e-mail their presentations to each other for review and critique.

Standards met in this activity...	
ACTFL Standards	ISTE NETS Standards
1.3, 2.1, 2.2, 3.1, 3.2, 4.2, 5.1, 5.2	I-A, III-A, VI-D

6
Desktop Publishing

Martha Castañeda and Rui Cheng

I have always felt uncomfortable with the e-cards, and nowadays it looks like there are fewer free e-cards available. Besides, there is so little you can do to make your card personal...You want to get creative and have a great final product? Well—get Publisher.

Sixth-grade Spanish teacher

Publisher in the Foreign Language Classroom

Communication in the contemporary world is empowered by technology. In our classrooms, we should incorporate the new tools that make communication different. One of these tools is Microsoft Publisher—it gives users the ability to produce different types of material for print and Web, incorporating text and visuals and choosing color and design. With Publisher, you and your students can create fast and easy projects applying target language knowledge and creativity.

For more information about the application, visit Microsoft's Web site at http://office. microsoft.com/home/office.aspx?assetid=FX01085794. Microsoft offers a free trial version of the software.

Just try this!

Getting Started: Using Templates

Step 1

♦ Open Microsoft Publisher. Go to **Start > Programs > Microsoft Publisher**

♦ A Choose **Greeting Cards** from the options given under **Wizard** in the left column.

Step 3

♦ Select the type of card that you would like. A pictorial representation will appear in the right-hand column.

Step 4

♦ Choose the template that is most suitable for your card. Double click on the card to start your publication.

Step 5

♦ A picture will appear on the front of the card. You may use this picture or change it by double clicking the picture to get other options. Hint: If you are a beginner, you may use the **Wizard** to guide you in the design of your first card.

Now you are getting it!

Writing and Editing Text

Publisher gives you the option of using the default text or writing your own text.

Step 1

♦ To use the default text, leave it as is. To write your own text, click on the text box and simply type over the text to replace it.

♦ Format your text! You can format the text using the **Formatting** toolbar, which is similar to the one you use in Microsoft Word. To change the color, size, or style of the text, highlight the text that you want to edit. Next, go to **Format > Font** and make desired changes.

Now try this:

Have your students create greeting cards using the target language. Students can select the template they want to use and create their own greeting cards in the target language. They can insert an appropriate picture and format the text to reflect their creativity. If you are teaching a language that uses additional characters or a non-Roman alphabet, you may apply the font you usually use when writing a Microsoft Word document.

You have got something to smile about!

Extension I—Inserting Images

♦ On the **Insert** menu, choose **Picture**. You may use one of the samples given by choosing **Clip Art**. Click on the **Insert** menu from the menu bar and choose **Picture > Clipart**.

♦ You may also choose to insert your own picture that you have saved on your hard drive. From the **Insert** menu, choose **Picture > From File**. Locate the file name and click **Insert**. Resize the picture by dragging the handle around the picture frame.

Extension II—Moving Pictures Around

♦ Pictures may be moved to another location on your card. Click on the picture, and when you see a small truck with the word **Move** on it, move the picture to the desired location on the card.

♦ You may also change the picture by double clicking on it to reveal other files. Replace the picture by choosing from the selections given.

- To change the color of the picture, click on that picture. On the **Format** menu, choose **Recolor Picture**. Choose the desired color and apply it to the picture.

- Now try to edit the text on the card you that you made in the previous activity. Change the font color, size, and type. Insert a clip art image or a picture saved to a file. Save the card.

Tricks and Traps

- Trick: Until you become comfortable working on your own, use the **Greeting Card Wizard** to guide you as you create your card.

Reflections

- What skills will you incorporate into the language learning process by using Microsoft Publisher?

- How could an application such as this motivate you and your students?

- How could you and your students share your published work with people outside the class? Do you think the opportunity to share a card created with peers will motivate them to use the target language?

Enjoy!

Activity 1: Let's Visit Places: Any Language

- Nature of the activity: Exploring the target language culture.

- Type of activity: Communicate about the target language country.

- Proficiency level: Beginners to advanced.

- Time: 20 minutes.

- Skills: Basic reading skills (if the students use online resources in the target language).

- Additional materials: Internet connection, search engines, Nicenet (see Chapter 12).

This activity can be assigned as an individual or a group project. Instruct your students to imagine that they are visiting the target language country. Ask them to create a card to mail home to their friends that highlights the interesting spots they have visited; they will need to include pictures of interesting places. You may instruct them to search on the Internet for images, or you can search for appropriate Web sites yourself and provide these links to the students (i.e., post the links on Nicenet; see Chapter 12).

Standards met in this activity...	
ACTFL Standards	ISTE NETS Standards
1.2, 2.1, 4.1, 4.2, 5.1	I-A, II-C, II-D, III-A, III-B, III-C

Activity 2: Celebrate With Your Pen Pal

♦ Nature of the activity: Writing communication.

♦ Type of activity: Writing to a pen pal.

♦ Proficiency level: Beginners to advanced.

♦ Time: 20 minutes.

♦ Skills: Basic writing skills in the target language.

♦ Additional materials: Internet connection, search engines, Nicenet (see Chapter 12).

Instruct your students to imagine that today is their pen pal's birthday. Ask them to create a card to congratulate him or her. Provide information about how birthdays are celebrated in the country. You may also provide them with culturally appropriate images to be used when creating the card, post Web sites on Nicenet (see Chapter 12), or ask them to search the Internet for images.

Standards met in this activity...	
ACTFL Standards	ISTE NETS Standards
1.2, 2.1, 4.1, 4.2, 5.1	I-A, II-C, II-D, III-A, III-B, III-C

Activity 3: Say Thank You!

♦ Nature of the activity: Writing communication.

♦ Type of activity: Writing to a friend.

♦ Proficiency level: Beginners to advanced.

♦ Time: 10 minutes.

♦ Skills: Basic writing skills in the target language.

♦ Additional materials: Internet connection, search engines, Nicenet (see Chapter 12).

Instruct your students to imagine that they have just returned from visiting a friend who lives in Franc, Germany, Spain, or another country. Ask students to send a card thanking the friend for allowing them to staying at his her house and for having a wonderful time while they were there.

Standards met in this activity...	
ACTFL Standards	**ISTE NETS Standards**
1.2, 2.1, 4.1, 4.2, 5.1	I-A, II-C, II-D, III-A, III-B, III-C

7
Creating Sound Files

Sabine Siekmann

I have always been interested in things that give life to the written word. Technology does that. I can add sounds, voices, music and lots and lots of pictures. My students love it when we read an online story.

Eighth-grade Japanese teacher

Sound Recording in the Foreign Language Classroom

Comprehensible input is arguably the most important element in the foreign language classroom. However, output is also crucial to developing proficiency, and ultimately, the goal is interaction. Using sound recording software targets all three areas. The teacher can record target language speech and music samples that are appropriate not only to students' proficiency level but also to their interests and learning goals. Digital sounds can be slowed down to make authentic speech or music more comprehensible. When students take over the microphone to create their own projects, sound recording allows them to develop oral proficiency. Interaction with other students can be fostered through collaborative projects, and in conjunction with e-mail, learners can send spoken messages to native speakers and receive them in return.

The use of authentic and teacher-created materials focuses mainly on the interpretational aspect of the communication standard, but it also allows students to gain an understanding of the practices and products of the target culture, as indicated in the cultures standard. Student-created projects target the expressive elements outlined in the communication standard but also provide opportunities to explore other content areas, as described in the connections standard. Both encourage the use of the language outside the classroom and foster lifelong learning, as indicated in the communities standard.

Many desktop and laptop computers have built-in microphones and speakers. However, the use of external microphones will improve the sound quality of your recordings, and speakers and headphones will enhance the quality of the playback. Headsets that combine a microphone and headphones are a cost-effective and space-saving option.

A large number of sound recording and editing programs are available for both PCs and Macs as free downloads (e.g., Audacity) or for purchase (e.g., Adobe Audition, Goldwave, Blazenet). This chapter discusses the functionality of Sound Recorder, a built-in component of all Windows operating systems for the PC. These steps will take you through the creation of a self-introduction with background music and sound effects.

Just try this!

Create a Voice Recording

Step 1   Setting up the speakers

First, make sure the speakers are plugged into the computer's sound card. Most computers have color-coded plug-ins marked with a headphone symbol on the back of the CPU. Many external speakers also need to be plugged into a power source. Finally, make sure that the sound on the computer is not muted. To check the status of the computer's sound, look at the icons on the lower right-hand side of your screen.

 indicates the sound is muted;   indicates the sound is not muted.

If the sound on the computer is muted, follow these steps:

♦ First, you may have to expand the system tray to show hidden icons. To do this, click on the white arrow.

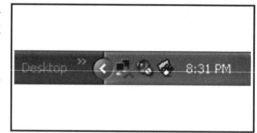

♦ To turn on the sound, right-click on the **Volume** icon.

♦ Select **Open Volume Control**.

♦ On the **Volume Control** menu, make sure the **Mute all** box is unchecked.

♦ Make sure the volume lever is set to a medium position.

To test the speakers, insert a music CD into the CD-ROM drive and start it; if everything is set up correctly, you should be able to hear the music you selected!

Step 2   Setting up the microphone

Most computers have built-in microphones, but an external microphone is necessary to record high-quality sound. External microphones are available in a range of prices, but for most classroom projects, even those at the lower end of the scale will be sufficient. However, if your budget allows it, it is a good idea to purchase USB microphones, as they are compatible with both PCs and Macs and generally produce a higher-quality recording.

First, make sure that the microphone is plugged into the computer's sound card. Most computers have a color-coded plug-in marked with a microphone symbol on the back of the CPU (and sometimes on the front as well). If you are using a USB microphone, plug it into one of the computer's USB ports. Finally, to make sure that the computer is set to record from the external microphone, follow these steps:

- Right-click on the **Volume** icon in the system tray and select **Open Volume Control**.

- Click on the **Options** menu and select **Properties**.

- Under **Adjust volume for**, select **Recording**. Make sure the check boxes next to both **CD Player** and **Microphone** are selected.

- Click **OK**.

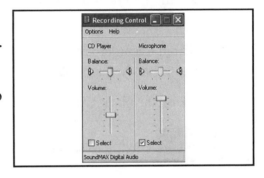

- Click on the **Select** box in the **Microphone** column.

The only way to test your microphone is to try to record a file. We will do this in the next section.

Step 3   Opening Sound Recorder

Sound Recorder is a basic sound recording and editing program that is part of any standard Windows installation. From the **Start** menu, select **Programs > Accessories > Entertainment > Sound Recorder**.

Sound Recorder has a very straightforward interface. Other sound recording and editing software programs have additional menus and options, but most have these basic features:

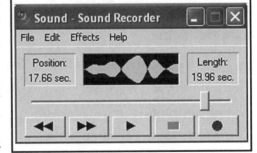

- The menu bar provides access to options and editing features.

- The position indicators allow you to find a particular point in a sound file.

- The wave form display area visually represents the sound in a recording.

- The length informs you of the duration of the file.

♦ Audio control buttons read from left to right: rewind, fast forward, start, stop, record.

Step 4 Recording a short self-introduction

Jot down a few words to guide you as you extemporaneously record two to three sentences about yourself, including a greeting, your name, your hometown, etc.

A tip before you start recording: Do not speak directly into the microphone. The microphone should be placed below your chin, about 10 inches from your mouth. This will prevent bursts of air hitting from the microphone.

♦ Click on the red **Record** button.

♦ Wait a few seconds.

♦ Introduce yourself in the target language.

♦ Keep the introduction to two or three sentences for now.

♦ If Sound Recorder is recording, you will see sound waves in the display window.

♦ Click on the black **Stop** button to stop recording.

Step 5 Saving your file

♦ On the **File** menu, select **Save as**.

♦ Choose a file location and write it down for future reference.

♦ Enter a file name (e.g., Sabineintro.wav).

♦ Click on **Save**.

Step 6a Listening to your file

♦ Click on the **Play** button to listen to your recording.

♦ Don't worry if your recording is not perfect—you will edit it in the next step.

♦ If you cannot hear your recording, double check your speakers and microphone. If all of your settings are correct, see the troubleshooting tips below.

Step 6b   Troubleshooting

If you are using a USB microphone, you might have to select it as the recording device in the **Control Panel**. To do this,

◆ Right-click on the **Volume** icon in the system tray on the lower right-hand side of the screen.

◆ Select **Adjust Audio Properties**.

◆ Select the **Voice** tab.

◆ Make sure the external microphone is selected. Click on the drop-down menu in the **Voice recording** section and choose a different default device.

◆ Click **OK**.

Now you are getting it!

Edit Your Voice Recording

Step 7   Deleting unwanted portions of your file

You probably have some silence at the beginning of your file, and you may even be able to hear yourself taking a deep breath before starting your self-introduction. All sound editing programs allow you to select and delete portions of the sound file. Sound Recorder, however, only allows you to delete unwanted portions at the beginning and end of a sound file.

◆ Listen to your file, watching the position indicator and the elapsed time, note when your self-introduction begins.

◆ Silence appears as a straight line in the wave form display, whereas peaks indicate recorded sounds. This visual display can be useful in identifying the beginning of words, phrases, and sentences.

◆ Place the position indicator at the start of your introduction by dragging the lever or pausing the sound file at that point.

♦ On the menu bar, select **Edit**.

♦ Choose **Delete Before Current Position**.

♦ Listen to your edited sound file.

♦ Save the sound file if you are happy with the change.

♦ If you wish to delete a portion at the end of the file, select **Delete After Current Position** instead.

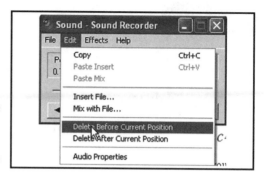

Step 8 Adding on to your file

You might want to add more information to your introduction—for example, some of your favorite pastimes. To do this, you can either add to this file or create a new file, which you will then append to the original.

Note: Sound Recorder allows you to record only up to 60 seconds (other programs do not have this limitation). Consequently, if plan to create longer files using Sound Recorder, you will need to string several sound files together.

In this section, you will add a few additional sentences at the end of your original file.

♦ Move the position indicator to the end of the file.

♦ Click on the **Record** button and talk about your hobbies.

♦ Click the **Stop** button to stop the recording.

♦ Click the **Play** button to listen to your extended file.

You can also add on to your introduction by creating a separate sound file, which is then inserted at the end of your original recording. This is a useful technique to use if you are combining recordings prepared by different students, as in the Morning Show activity described later in this chapter. This allows each student or group of students to record and perfect their own portion before combining them into the final project.

To create a new file,

♦ Open a new Sound Recorder file by clicking on the **File** menu and selecting **New**.

♦ Record the second part of your self-introduction.

♦ Save this file with a different file name (e.g., "intropart2").

♦ Open the first part of your self-introduction.

♦ Move the position indicator to the end of the file.

- On the **Edit** menu, select **Insert File**.

- Navigate to and select the second part of your self-introduction.

- Click on **Open**.

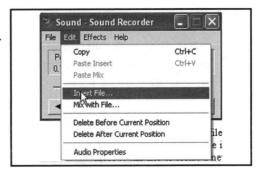

Tip: You can also download sound effects from the Internet and insert them into a sound file.

Step 9 Recording from a CD

You may also want to record sounds from a CD. In our example, you will record some music to use as a background to our self-introduction. Identify a piece of music, preferably one without lyrics, that reflects your personality.

Recording from a CD is useful if you are using music in the classroom, as in the Fill-in-the-Blank Song activity described later in this chapter. Recording portions of songs allows you to navigate quickly to the particular song and location you are using. (*Reminder:* Whenever you are using copyrighted materials, be sure to observe copyright laws.)

Step 10 Changing the recording options to CD

Thus far, you have been recording through the microphone. Now, you'll need to change the recording option from the microphone to the CD.

- Right-click on the **Volume** icon in the system tray and select **Open Volume Control**.

- Click on the **Options** menu and select **Properties**.

- Under **Adjust volume for**, select **Recording**.

- Click **OK**.

- Click on **Select** in the **CD Player** column.

Step 11 Starting the CD and recording your selection

- Open a new file in Sound Recorder.

- Insert a music CD into the CD-ROM drive of your computer; the CD should launch automatically.

- In Sound Recorder, click the **Record** button.

- In the CD player interface, select **Start the CD**.

- Click the **Stop** button in Sound Recorder at the end of your selection.

- Save the file with a new name (e.g., "background").

- Remember you can only record 60 seconds in Sound Recorder, which is long enough for this introduction and generally sufficient if you are focusing on a particular element in a song.

You have got something to smile about!

Mixing Your Voice With Music

Now you will combine the introduction and the background music, and you might even want to add a sound effect.

Step 12 Mixing with recorded music

- Open the file with your self-introduction.

- Move the position indicator to the beginning of the file.

- Select **Edit > Mix with File**.

- Navigate to and select the file containing your background music.

- Click on **Open**.

- Save your file.

Step 13 Downloading and inserting sound effects

Many sound effects, such as applause, ring tones, and nature sounds, are available for free downloading on the Internet. Adding them to your self-introduction can add interest and reflect your personality.

- Locate sound effects by searching the Internet with the key words "sound effects"

- Right-click on the file name.

- Select **Save target as**.

- Choose a location and save the file.

Follow the steps described earlier to insert the sound effect or mix it with your existing file.

Final Touches

Step 14 Slowing down

In many sound editing programs, it is possible to slow down recorded speech. Unfortunately, this generally distorts the message. To slow down speech using Sound Recorder,

♦ Click on the **Effect** menu and select **Decrease Speed**.

Step 15 Choosing recording options

All sound recorders and editors allow you to record at different settings and change the file format. The two important factors in sound recording are sound quality and file size: the better the sound quality, the larger the file size. You need to find the right balance because storage space is usually limited, and large files take a long time to load on the Internet.

♦ Click on the **File** menu.

♦ Select **Properties**.

♦ Next to the **Choose from: All formats** drop-down menu, click on **Convert Now**.

♦ Click on the **Attributes** drop-down menu.

♦ For most classroom projects, there is no need to record in stereo, as you are using only one microphone.

You can also use this menu to convert your .wav file into another format. The most commonly used format is MPEG because these files are smaller. To change to this format, click on the **Format** drop-down menu and select **MPEG-Layer 3**.

Tricks and Traps

♦ **Trap:** Sound Recorder only allows you to record 60 seconds at a time.

• **Trick:** Although 60 seconds is sufficient for most classroom projects, you can record several individual files, which can then be combined to create longer files.

♦ **Trap:** File sizes of longer recordings are too large.

• **Trick:** Sound Recorder creates .wav files, which does not require any special software for playback. This makes them very versatile; however, the trade-off is that file sizes tend to be large if your file is longer than a few seconds. If you are using a CD to store and play your sound files, this should not be a problem. However, if you need to reduce the file size because you want to use your files on the Internet, you can convert them to MP3 files within Sound Recorder, or you can use another program to convert them into other Web-compatible formats (e.g., .mov, .rm).

- **Trap:** The background music is too loud in comparison to your recorded voice.

  - **Trick:** Choose **Decrease Volume** on the **Effects** menu.

Reflections

- How can spoken language samples improve my students' listening comprehension, linguistic awareness, and cultural knowledge?

- How can sound recording stimulate my students' creativity?

- How can sound recording assist my students' oral production?

- Can sound recording provide opportunities for student-to-student interactions?

Gone are the days of purely repetitive language lab listening and speaking exercises—they are too formulaic and do not allow for student creativity. However, students still benefit from hearing spoken language samples, especially if they are authentic and reflect cultural content in the target language. Existing listening materials might not cover certain content areas, but teacher-created sound files can be tailored to your students' needs and allow for the incorporation of different dialects and accents. Additionally, the use of music can lower students' anxiety levels and fosters the use of multiple intelligences.

By recording and carefully listening to their own speech, students are put in a position to notice the gap between their output and target utterances. Moreover, creating sound projects fosters students' creativity and language play and helps students make connections with other content areas, fellow students, and even native speakers.

Enjoy!

Activity 1: Where Am I?

- Nature of the activity: Students listen to target language recordings by a variety of speakers using different dialects.

- Type of activity: This activity can be conducted in a whole class, small group, or individual setting. If performed individually, students can listen to the recording as often as necessary and work on intensive listening skills; if it is conduced in a small group or with the whole class, students can discuss clues.

- ◆ Proficiency level: Advanced beginning to advanced fluency level.

- ◆ Time: 5–15 minutes, depending on the length of the recording and the amount of discussion.

- ◆ Skills: Listening and speaking skills in the target language, as well as culture.

- ◆ Additional materials: CD player or computer(s) with speakers.

Prior to the activity, the teacher collects several target language recordings of place descriptions, either by native speakers with different dialects or by other language teachers. The teacher then plays the recording(s) for the students, who must figure out where the speaker is located. Clues might include geographic information, famous sights, or traditions. Variations in pronunciation will familiarize students with different dialects. If necessary, the teacher can assist students with unknown words, but the focus should be on identifying only crucial information.

This activity could be expanded to include reading and writing skills by providing students with a printout of the text after listening to the recording. Students could then also be asked to write (and record) a description of their own hometown.

Standards met in this activity...	
ACTFL Standards	ISTE NETS Standards
1.2, 2.2, 3.2	I -A, I-D, II–B, II-D

Activity 2: Fill-in-the-Blank Song

- ◆ Nature of the activity: Students listen to a target language song and try to fill in missing words in the lyrics.

- ◆ Type of activity: This activity can be conducted in a whole class, small group, or individual setting. If performed individually, students can listen to the recording as often as necessary and work on intensive listening skills; if it is conduced in a small group or with the whole class, students can work together to understand missing words.

- ◆ Proficiency level: Beginning to advanced fluency level.

- ◆ Time: 10–20 minutes, depending on the length of the recording.

- ◆ Skills: Listening and reading skills in the target language, as well as culture.

- ◆ Additional materials: CD player or computer(s) with speakers, printer.

Prior the activity, the teacher records a clip from a song in the target language. Depending on the age of the students, the song could be a children's song, a folk song, or a pop song. The song should include frequent repetition, use conversational language, and be fairly easy to comprehend. The song might also be selected based on the types of structures it contains. The teacher types the lyrics into a word processing program but replaces key words or phrases with blanks. It is important not to use too many blanks so as to give students enough contextual support, as well as enough time to write down the words and phrases while the song is playing. This worksheet is then printed for each student.

During class, the teacher introduces the song and the artist and plays the selection for the class without providing the lyrics. Depending on the student's proficiency level, the teachers asks students whether there were any words they were able to understand (beginners), or whether there were any words they didn't know (intermediate and advanced). Students at all levels can guess what they think the song is about, but the discussion will go into greater depth at the more advanced levels.

The teacher hands out the worksheet and gives the students a few minutes to look at the lyrics. Depending on the students' level, the teacher might answer questions about unknown vocabulary. The teacher plays the song once or twice more as students try to fill in the missing words and phrases. Depending on the students' level of proficiency, the teacher can read the lyrics and ask students to shout out the missing words while writing them on the blackboard (beginning and low intermediate), or students can take turns reading the lyrics. The selected portion of the song is played once or twice more while the class and the teacher sing along.

As an extension, after filling in the complete lyrics, students could discuss the meaning of the song, write a new verse, or rewrite the chorus. These activities allow students to focus on creative speaking and writing skills.

Standards met in this activity...	
ACTFL Standards	**ISTE NETS Standards**
1.2, 2.1, 3.2, 4.2, 5.2	I-A, I-D, II-B, II-D

Activity 3: Self-Introductions

♦ Nature of the activity: Students record a self-introduction to share with their peers, family, or e-mail exchange pals.

♦ Type of activity: In this activity, each students needs access to a computer equipped with a microphone and sound recording software. However, if computers are not available for all students, students can take turns using the equipment that is available.

♦ Proficiency level: Beginning to intermediate fluency level.

♦ Time: 5–10 minutes per student.

- ◆ Skills: Speaking skills in the target language, as well as culture.

- ◆ Additional materials: Computer(s) equipped with microphone, headphones, and sound recording software.

This activity works well as a culminating project at the end of a unit in which students have learned to state their name, age, hometown, and hobbies, as well as appropriate ways to introduce oneself in the target culture.

Students review key phrases and receive assistance with unknown vocabulary. Students write down key phrases to help them during their recording, but they should be encouraged to speak extemporaneously. Students record a short self-introduction and save it in a designated location. Then they listen to their own recordings and have the opportunity to edit them until they have created a recording they are satisfied with. The teacher provides individualized feedback to each student regarding cultural appropriateness, grammatical accuracy, and pronunciation. Students should be able to take their recordings home to share with their families.

Variation: Who Am I?

In this variation, instead of recording a self-introduction, students describe themselves so that other students in the class can guess who they are. Information might include a description of their physical appearance (e.g., "I am tall, have blue eyes, and short brown hair."), as well as a description of clothing (e.g., "I am wearing a red sweater, blue jeans, and white tennis shoes."). The teacher then plays the recordings to the class, and students guess who is speaking.

Extension: Voice E-Mail Exchange

This introduction can also be used as the first message that students send in a voice e-mail exchange. The teacher locates a group of similar age native speakers of the target language or another foreign language class with whom students can exchange messages in the target language.

Standards met in this activity...	
ACTFL Standards	**ISTE NETS Standards**
1.3, 2.1, 3.2, 5.2	I-A, I-D, II-B, II-D

Activity 4: The Foreign Language Morning Show

- ◆ Nature of the activity: Students create a radio program in the target language.

- ◆ Type of activity: In this activity, students should work in small groups to plan, write, record, and edit different portions of a morning news show. All of the elements will then be combined to create a complete project.

- Proficiency level: Intermediate to superior fluency.

- Time: Several class periods, depending on the complexity of the program.

- Skills: Listening, reading, speaking, and writing skills in the target language, as well as culture.

- Additional materials: Computer(s) equipped with microphone, headphones, and sound recording software.

Prior to the activity students, may have been exposed to radio or television programs in the target language or culture. Students brainstorm ideas about the types of segments they want to include in their morning show. Possible segments might be news, weather, entertainment news, interviews, and songs. You may want your students to visit http://www.languagebox.com/ Resources.htm, a Web resource for foreign language newspapers, magazines, television, radio, dictionaries, and more.

Students form groups to work on individual segments. Each group writes a script for their segment. Students should be encouraged to consult current target language sources (e.g., on the Internet) to find out who and what is currently in the news, what the weather is going to be, what sporting events are coming up, and so on.

Students record and edit their segments, and all of the segments are compiled into one program. This program could be broadcast to other students and should also be available for students to share with their families.

Standards met in this activity...	
ACTFL Standards	ISTE NETS Standards
1.1, 1.3, 2.1, 3.1, 3.2, 4.2, 5.2	I-A, I-D, II-B, II-D

Activity 5: My (Audio) Learning Portfolio

- Nature of the activity: Throughout the semester, students compile projects (including those for which they have created sound files) onto a CD to trace their progress and share with their families.

- Type of activity: This activity is carried out over the course of the semester and gives all students an opportunity to create a lasting artifact of their target language learning. Not only does this allow family members to gain insights into students' developing proficiency, but also students can trace their own progress.

- Proficiency level: Advanced beginning to advanced fluency.

- Time: Varies depending on the number of projects.

- Skills: Listening, reading, speaking, and writing skills in the target language, as well as culture.

♦ Additional materials: Computer(s) equipped with CD burner, microphone, headphones, and sound recording and editing software, as well as a CD for each student.

Students collect language learning artifacts throughout the semester. At a very basic level, these files may simply be stored on a computer or network until students burn them to CD. For a more comprehensive portfolio, students might want to link projects together in a hyperlinked document, a PowerPoint presentation, or a word processing document. Additionally, reflective pieces of writing might be included (why certain projects were selected for the portfolio, how particular artifacts showcase a new skills, etc.).

Standards met in this activity...	
ACTFL Standards	ISTE NETS Standards
Depending on the type of portfolio and projects involved, this activity can address all standards.	I-A, I-D, II-B, II-D

8
Video Streaming: iMovie and Movie Maker

Rui Cheng and Robert Summers

I have seen many things on TV and wished I could create them in my class with my students…now I can, with moviemaking software. My students and I have created lots of shows; fashion shows, news reports etc. All were great fun and my students were using their foreign language while doing their shows.

Ninth-grade German teacher

iMovie and Movie Maker in the Foreign Language Classroom

The software package iMovie is a video editing program created by Apple. Its PC counterpart is Movie Maker. Both programs enable users to edit their own movies easily. Apple's iMovie has been widely used since its introduction to the market, and Movie Maker quickly gained popularity among PC users. These programs are known for their simplicity—most tasks can be accomplished simply by dragging or dropping. For this reason, they are widely used in educational settings, even among elementary school students. In the recent years, movie making has been adopted by foreign language teachers as a tool to promote communication. Foreign language students can shoot movies for a role-play activity in the target language or edit a movie by applying the target language. Just imagine your students making a news report and then putting it onto a Web site or filming a play and then editing it with voice-overs and sound. Better yet, imagine your students creating a virtual tour of a famous tourist attraction in the target country and then recording simultaneous commentary.

Part I: Using iMovie

Just try this!

To apply iMovie effectively in the foreign language classroom, you'll first need to become familiar with how it works. What follows are detailed descriptions for using iMovie software. After you know the working mechanisms of this software, you can extend your imagination to use it in as many ways as possible.

♦ First, shoot a short video that you edit using iMovie. You can film just about anything (e.g., a role-play activity in the target language) using a digital video camera.

♦ Transfer the video from your digital video camera to your computer using a cable.

♦ Launch the iMovie software from the computer you are using to produce the movie.

♦ Open the movie project in the iMovie software. When the movie project opens, you'll see your digital video clips on the "shelf" to the right of the screen. The shelf is a temporary storage area for clips that you plan to use in the movie. All of the clips from the video that you shot will be stored here during this stage.

♦ To select particular clips to include in your movie, click on these on the shelf.

♦ Drag the selected clip from the shelf to the clip viewer at the bottom of the screen. To select multiple clips at once, hold down the **Shift** key, click on the clips you wish to select, and drag them together to the clip viewer.

♦ To arrange the clips in a different order in the clip viewer, click on the **Edit** menu, choose **Select None**, and drag the video clips to the desired positions in the clip viewer. The clips stay in place until you release the mouse button.

Now you are getting it!

You've learned how to prepare the video that you shot for editing. Now, it's time to get your feet wet. Try the following steps, and see whether you can do all of them. Then review and practice.

- Film a role-play about shopping for books in the target language in the classroom.

- Transfer the video to your computer.

- Drag all of the clips you are plan to use onto the clip viewer and click **Play**.

- Rearrange the order of the clips if you're not satisfied with your movie.

You have got something to smile about!

During the editing process, if you find that some portions of the video are not necessary for the movie, you can easily delete them. To delete extra video, follow these steps:

- Click and drag the cursor just below the scrubber bar under the iMovie monitor. Crop marks will appear. (The scrubber bar is the bar above which you have dragged all your movie clips.)

- Drag the beginning crop mark and end crop mark to the place where you would like to cut.

- On the **Edit** menu, choose **Clear**.

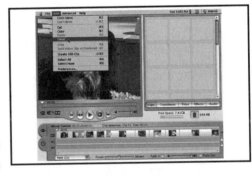

In other circumstances, you might want to split a video clip. To split a video, follow these steps:

- Select the clip you want to split in the clip viewer.

- On the scrubber bar, drag the playhead to the place you want to split. (The playhead is the cursor line that moves along the scrubber bar when the movie is playing.)

- On the **Edit** menu, choose **Split Video Clip at Playhead**.

Now it's time for another round of practice. Do you know now how to delete and split your video? If so, go ahead and try the following activities. If not, go back to the previous section and review the procedures.

- Delete clips or parts of clips that you think are unnecessary (e.g., any long pause).

- Split the clip and choose the part you want and delete the part you don't want.

Sometimes, you don't just want to make a movie—you want to produce a good movie. You may want to add video effects and transitions or give the movie a snappy title so that you can find it easily later. Follow these instructions to add video effects, transitions, and titles to your movie.

It is not difficult to add video effects to a movie. In the following example, you will add an effect between the two clips of video. Once you learn how to do it, you can add many types of effects to any clip. To add video effects, follow these steps:

- ◆ Select the first two clips in the clip viewer.

- ◆ Click **Effects**.

- ◆ Select **Sepia Tone** (one of the effects that you can choose from) on the **Effects** panel.

- ◆ To see what this effect will look like before you apply it to your movie, click the **Preview** button on the **Effects** panel to see a preview of the effect in the iMovie monitor.

- ◆ Click **Apply** to finishing adding the effect.

The next skill that you are going to learn is adding transitions. You will be amazed at how good your movie looks after adding transitions. To add a transition, follow these steps:

- ◆ Click the **Transitions** button.

- ◆ Adjust the **Speed** slider to the appropriate position.

- ◆ Drag the **Overlap** transition (one of the transitions that you can choose from) from the list on the Transitions panel and insert it between two clips in the clip viewer.

- ◆ Preview the transition.

The last skill that you are going to learn is adding titles. It is always a good idea to give your movie a title. It not only shows care for your project but also provides you with the convenience of finding this movie later. To add a title to your movie, follow these steps:

- ◆ Click the second clip in the clip viewer.

- ◆ Click the **Titles** button.

- ◆ Adjust the **Speed** slider on the **Titles** panel.

- ◆ Scroll through the title list and select **Typewriter**.

- ◆ Make the text larger by dragging the **Text Size** slider all the way to the right.

- ◆ In the text fields at the bottom of the **Titles** panel, type the title.

- Drag the **Typewriter** title from the style list and place it in front of the second clip in the clip viewer.

- On the **Edit** menu, choose **Select None**, then select the third clip in the clip viewer and press **Delete**.

- Preview the title.

- Save all of your work before exiting the program.

Are you eager to create a movie yourself now that you have learned so many skills in such a short period of time? Perform the following tasks one by one. If you forget one or more, you can always go back to the previous instructions. Good luck making your own movie!

- Add a title to your movie.

- Add video effects to your movie.

- Add several transitions to your movie.

- Show the movie to the whole class.

Tricks and Traps

- **Trap:** It seems that iMovie technology is not as simple as iImage. How can I be sure my students will learn it quickly, as they are young learners?

  - **Trick:** Real-world experience has proved that kids learn iMovie software as fast as adults—or even faster! Good instruction and playing to their interests are key to the successful application of iMovie in the foreign language classroom. Help is everywhere. Teachers can register for workshops or self-learn through online tutorials. If you don't feel confident introducing iMovie to your students, invite a guest speaker to help you accomplish the task.

- **Trap:** Sure, iMovie is fun, and I know my students will love it. But how can I make sure they stay focused on foreign language learning rather than the fun part of the technology?

  - **Trick**: This is a challenging task for teachers. Constantly reminding students that they should focus on foreign language learning tasks is necessary, but not enough. Teachers should work on the tasks assigned to the students. That is to say, the teachers needs to find tasks that closely connect iMovie technology with foreign language learning. In this way, the process of producing a movie is also the process of learning a foreign language.

- **Trap:** There are many different functions in the iMovie software, such as effects, transitions, and so on. Which functions should I ask students to include in their movies?

- **Trick:** There is no definite answer about what to include or not include in the movies that students produce. It depends on the foreign language learning tasks that you want students to accomplish. Although it is better for students to know as many functions as possible, that is not the main purpose of the lesson. The main purpose is always for students to master the foreign language concepts through the activities they perform.

- ♦ **Trap:** It seems time-consuming to complete an iMovie activity. Is there an individual activity or group activity that uses iMovie to learn a foreign language?

- **Trick:** Again, there is no definite answer. Teachers can decide how tasks should be finished according to the real classroom situation. In many cases, performing an iMovie task is time-consuming and difficult for a student to finish successfully. In that case, working in a group might be a better idea. Students in the group can take different roles. They can share their ideas and help each other when they encounter difficulty.

Part II: Using Movie Maker

Just try this!

Let's explore Movie Maker now, this time performing a different task than the one presented in the first section of this chapter. We will explore the steps for making an animated collection of pictures with voice-over commentaries.

Step 1

- ♦ Open Movie Maker and click on **Import pictures** on the **Movie Tasks** menu. A dialogue box will ask you to browse for the pictures that you want to import. Choose the pictures you want to import and click **OK**. The imported picture will appear in the bin.

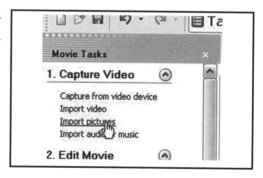

Step 2

♦ Now that your pictures are in the bin (similar to the shelf in iMovie), drag them onto the storyboard in the order that you want them to appear.

♦ Make sure that you are looking at the storyboard, not the timeline view. The buttons, detailed in the images below, toggle from view to view.

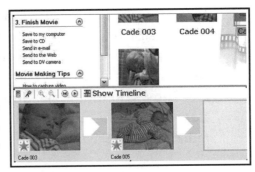

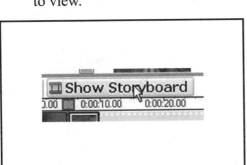 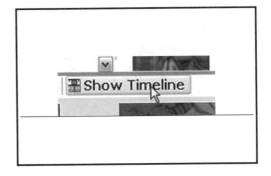

Step 3

♦ After adding all of the pictures that you have imported, add transitions if you wish. On the **Edit** menu, select **View Video Transitions** and choose a transition by dragging it onto the storyboard. You can preview the transition in the video window at the right of the screen.

Step 4

♦ You can also add a video effect to the pictures. To do this, select **View Video Effects** from the **Edit** menu. Drag an effect from the bin and place it over the picture that you want to enhance.

Step 5

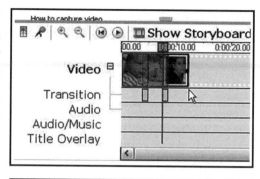

♦ When you have arranged all of your pictures, transitions, and video effects, you might want to adjust the timing of your slides and transitions. Do this by toggling the **Show Timeline** and **Show Storyboard** buttons. Your view will change to reflect the image to the right.

♦ The default view is somewhat compact. Zoom in on the timeline so that it is easier to lengthen clips. To do this, click on the magnifying glass until the timeline expands.

Step 6

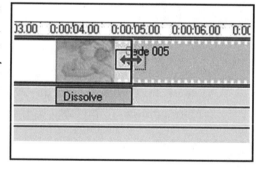

♦ In the expanded timeline view, increase the length of your clips by selecting a clip and clicking on it. A double-headed red arrow will appear when you hover over the edge of your clip. Click, hold, and drag the clip to the desired length. You can also extend the length of transitions.

Step 7

♦ You can import audio into your movie in the same way that you imported pictures into the bin. Click **Import Audio or Music** in the **Movie Tasks** menu.

◆ After you have imported the audio, drag it onto the timeline at the bottom of the screen.

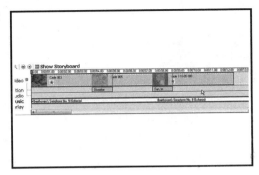

◆ There may be some overlap between the audio and video. To remove audio that continues after the video finishes, move the playhead (shown in blue) to the beginning of the audio portion that you wish to remove. On the menu bar, select **Clip > Split**. Next, select the part of the audio that you wish to remove and hit **Delete**.

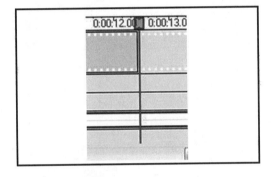

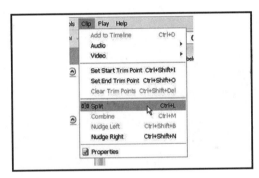

◆ To fade the audio in or out, select the audio by clicking on it. Right-click and select **Fade In** or **Fade Out**.

Now you are getting it!

Step 11

♦ When your video is finished, it must be rendered. This process mixes the audio and video tracks into one file. At any time, you can preview your movie in the window on the right side of the screen. To render your movie, select **Save to My Computer** under **Finish Movie**.

Step 12

♦ Select a location in which your movie will be saved and choose the quality of the file. Remember, the higher the quality, the larger the file.

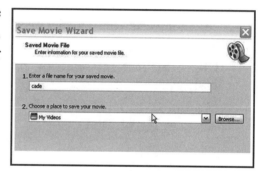

Step 13

♦ Generally the default Windows setting for saving a movie works best for videos created for the classroom. However, you can save your movie as a higher-quality file if you wish. If your computer is equipped with a DVD burner, you can even create a DVD that can be played in any DVD player.

Step 14

♦ Depending on the size of your movie, it may take a few minutes for it to be rendered. Be patient, and don't do anything thing else on the computer while this process is taking place. It requires a lot of the processor, and using system resources needlessly might result in a poor-quality video.

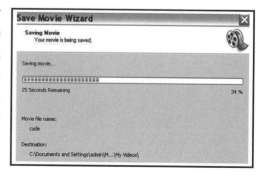

Reflections

♦ How can spoken language samples improve my students' listening comprehension, linguistic awareness, and cultural knowledge?

♦ How can sound recording stimulate my students' creativity?

♦ How can sound recording assist my students' oral production?

♦ Can sound recording provide opportunities for student-to-student interactions?

Gone are the days of purely repetitive listening and speaking exercises in the language lab —they are too formulaic and do not allow for student creativity. However, students still benefit from hearing spoken language samples, especially if they are authentic and reflect cultural content in the target language. Existing listening materials might not cover certain content areas, but teacher-created sound files can be tailored to your students' needs and allow for the incorporation of different dialects and accents. Additionally, the use of music can lower students' anxiety and foster the use of multiple intelligences.

By recording and carefully listening to their own speech, students are put in a position to notice the gap between their output and target utterances. Moreover, creating sound projects fosters students' creativity and language play and helps students make connections with other content areas, fellow students, and even native speakers.

Enjoy!

Activity 1: Where Am I?

♦ Nature of the activity: Students listen to target language recordings by a variety of speakers using different dialects.

♦ Type of activity: This activity can be conducted in a whole class, small group, or individual setting. If performed individually, students can listen to the recording as often as necessary and work on intensive listening skills; if it is conducted in small group or with the whole class, students can discuss clues.

♦ Proficiency level: Advanced beginning to advanced fluency.

♦ Time: 5–15 minutes, depending on the length of the recording and the amount of discussion.

♦ Skills: Listening and speaking skills in the target language, as well as culture.

♦ Additional materials: CD player or computer(s) with speakers.

Prior to the activity, the teacher collects several target language recordings of place descriptions, either by native speakers with different dialects or by other language teachers.

The teacher then plays the recording(s) for the students, who must figure out where the speaker is located. Clues might include geographic information, famous sights, or traditions. Variations in pronunciation will familiarize students with different dialects. If necessary, the teacher can assist students with unknown words, but the focus should be on identifying only crucial information.

This activity could be expanded to include reading and writing skills by providing students with a printout of the text after listening to the recording. Students could then also be asked to write and record a description of their own hometown.

Standards met in this activity...	
ACTFL Standards	ISTE NETS Standards
1.2, 2.2, 3.2	I-A, I-D, II-B, II-D

Activity 2: My Dream Vacation

♦ Nature of the activity: Students create a presentation.

♦ Type of activity: Individual or group activity.

♦ Proficiency level: All levels.

♦ Time: Ongoing.

♦ Skills: Reading, writing, listening, and speaking skills of thematic vocabulary.

♦ Additional materials: Current text or syllabus materials; current vocabulary; previous projects completed in class.

After introducing the appropriate vocabulary words for vacation, brainstorm with students about places they would like to visit. Use travel planning Web sites that are appropriate to the language you teach (e.g., there are both French and German versions of Expedia) to help students create an itinerary for their trip. Next, have students collect pictures, using Google's image search, to illustrate their dream vacation. Using the pictures they have gathered from the Internet, have students create a movie that depicts their vacation, adding captions, credits, and special effects if they wish. Next, using audio recording tools (see Chapter 7), students should narrate their movie in the target language. Remember, it is easier to create smaller sound clips and combine them than to create one long sound recording without interruptions.

Standards met in this activity...	
ACTFL Standards	ISTE NETS Standards
1.1, 1.3, 2.1, 2.2, 3.1, 3.2, 4.2, 5.1, 5.2	I-A, I-D, II-B, II-D

Activity 3: The News From Our School

♦ Nature of the activity: Students create a newscast.

♦ Type of activity: Group activity.

♦ Proficiency level: Intermediate to advanced.

♦ Time: Ongoing.

♦ Skills: Reading, writing, listening, and speaking skills of thematic vocabulary

♦ Additional materials: Current text or syllabus materials; current vocabulary

Speak with students about current events at your school. Perhaps there is a football game this weekend. Create a plan of what you want to address in your newscast. Storyboarding is a great way to organize your ideas and plan what you want your newscast to showcase.

Using a digital video recorder, record your newscast. Import your video into the movie editing software, edit it, and add captions and credits. Be sure that students conduct any interviews and provide reports in the target language. Share and showcase your newscasts with your students and colleagues. Newscasts from previous years can be used to trigger conversation about changes in the school.

Standards met in this activity...	
ACTFL Standards	**ISTE NETS Standards**
1.2,1.3, 2.1, 3.1, 3.2, 4.1, 4.2, 5.1, 5.2	I-A, I-D, II-B, II-D

Activity 4: Nice to Meet You

♦ Nature of the activity: Students create a presentation.

♦ Type of activity: Individual activity.

♦ Proficiency level: Beginning to intermediate.

♦ Time: Ongoing.

♦ Skills: Writing, listening, and speaking skills of thematic vocabulary

♦ Additional materials: Current text or syllabus materials; current vocabulary

After practicing introductions, ask your students to outline the things they might want to say to people when first meeting them. Using a digital video, pictures from a digital camera, or pictures gathered from the Internet, have students create individual introductions. Add titles, captions, and credits as appropriate. Require as much or as little information depending on the students' proficiency level. Showcase these movies in your class. You can even collect these activities from previous classes and use them in your lessons.

Standards met in this activity...	
ACTFL Standards	**ISTE NETS Standards**
1.1, 1.2, 1.3, 2.2, 3.1, 3.2, 4.2, 5.1, 5.2	I-A, I-D, II-B, II-D

Activity 5: Ordering a Meal

♦ Nature of the activity: Creative collaborative work.

♦ Type of activity: This is a group activity. The goal is for students to become familiar with the vocabulary used to order food in a restaurant in the target language and to become aware of the cultural aspects of dining at a restaurant.

♦ Proficiency level: Advanced beginning to advanced fluency.

♦ Time: This activity can start in class and be complete as a homework assignment. This activity will take a whole class session to shoot and edit the movies. The rest of the work can be done after class among group members; this work can take much longer, depending on how the students work together.

♦ Skills: Listening and speaking in the target language.

♦ Additional materials: Textbook.

Assign students to play the roles of waiter (or waitress), customer, and camera operator. Have the students rehearse and get ready to shoot the video. The students start the role-play activity, and the camera operator shoots the video. As a group, students transfer the video to a computer and use movie making software (iMovie or Movie Maker) to produce a movie. Once the project is done, show the movie to the whole class. The teacher and peers should evaluate the target language used in the role-play and the quality of the movie.

Standards met in this activity...	
ACTFL Standards	**ISTE NETS Standards**
1.1, 1.2, 1.3, 2.1, 2.2, 3.2, 5.1	II-A, II-D, II-E, III-A, III-B, III-C, III-D, IV-A

Activity 6: Introducing Your School

♦ Nature of the activity: Collaborative activity.

♦ Type of activity: This can be a whole-class activity.

♦ Proficiency level: Advanced beginning to advanced fluency.

- ◆ Time: This activity can be done in two to three class sessions or extended as a homework assignment. The whole project should be completed in one week.

- ◆ Skills: Reading, writing, listening, and speaking in the target language.

- ◆ Additional materials: Dictionary.

Together with your students, decide which aspects of your school will be covered in the movie. Then, ask the students to pick an interesting part to work on. Students can be divided into several groups, and each group can focus on one aspect of the school project. Within each group, students can further divide the tasks: Some might be responsible for writing the script, others might act in the movie, and others will be responsible for shooting the video. Group members will be working together to edit the video. Representatives of each group will bring each piece of the movie together. The movie can be sent to peers in another country.

Standards met in this activity...	
ACTFL Standards	**ISTE NETS Standards**
1.1, 1.2, 1.3, 3.1, 5.1, 5.2	II-A, II-D, II-E, III-C, III-D, V-C, V-D, VI-E

Section III

E-Communication

9

Listservs: Joining Communities

Rui Cheng and Martha Castañeda

Being in a school where I am the only Spanish teacher I sometimes feel isolated. However, since discovering Listservs I can ask or share anything with other foreign language teachers and I get immediate feedback.... They are my virtual colleagues.

Sixth-grade Spanish teacher

Listservs in the Foreign Language Classroom

Listservs are a formidable tool for promoting communication in the foreign language classroom. For many years, Listservs have been used all over the world by groups of people who have similar interests. In these Listservs, members discuss topics of concern by e-mail in their native languages. Foreign language professionals who participated in these original discussions perceived the potential of Listservs in the foreign language classroom. Listservs could be used by foreign language teachers and students to interact in the target language.

Specifically, a Listserv allows you and your students to submit questions and information to all the members of the Listserv by e-mail. To send an e-mail to the entire class, you enter only the e-mail address of the Listserv, and all Listserv members will receive that message. In this way, the Listservs can assist and facilitate whole-class or small-group e-mail discussions in the target language. You can create a Listserv just for your class. There are two ways to participate in a Listserv. You and your students can create your own Listserv using readily available software, or you can participate in discussions using already established Listservs.

If you choose to participate in an established Listserv, you will first need to subscribe to the Listserv. Once you subscribe to a Listserv, you will begin receiving e-mails from the Listserv. You can submit queries or comments of your own to the Listserv, but before doing so, it is a good idea to monitor the interaction of the list for a brief period of time to familiarize yourself with the culture of the Listserv. This is called "lurking." If you choose to create your own Listserv, you will find detailed instructions here.

Just try this!

Creating a Listserv

Step 1 Setting up a Listserv

Launch an Internet browser such as Netscape or Internet Explorer. Enter the address for Topica, http://lists.topica.com/index.html, in the address bar. Topica is a service that assists you in creating a Listserv. We selected the Topica Listserv service because it does not require any downloads, but there are many other services available. These are a few other sites that provide free Listserv services.

- http://www.greatcircle.com/majordomo/

- http://groups.yahoo.com/start

- http://www.lsoft.com/

- http://www.ossp.org/pkg/tool/petidomo/

- http://sourceforge.net/projects/listproc/

On the Topica Web site, click on **Discussion Lists—Connect for Free!** You will be directed to the registration or login site. If you are visiting this site for the first time, you will need to register. Click **Sign Me Up!** button at the bottom of the page and enter the information requested. The Topica site will ask you to enter basic information in order to set up the Listserv.

Now that you have registered, you are ready to create a Listserv. Click on **Start a List**.

You will be asked to enter basic information about your Listserv, such as a name and a description. Once your Listserv is registered, you will receive a welcome message from Topica. This message will provide you with your Listserv e-mail address.

Now you are getting it!

Step 2 Inviting members to the list

Now that you have created a Listserv, the next step is to invite members to join the list. In this case, you can invite the students from your class. You will be taken to a page with two text areas: **Create and Customize Message** and **Invite People to Join Your List**.

In the **Create a Customized Message** text area, you can compose a welcome message to new Listserv members. In the **Invite People to Join Your List** text area, you can enter the e-mail addresses of the students you would like to join your Listserv. Topica will automatically send an e-mail message to each student you invite. This message allows students to accept or decline the invitation to join the Listserv. Inform your students that they will be receiving this e-mail and that they need to accept the invitation in order to join the Listserv.

You have got something to smile about!

Post a message to the Listserv to elicit a discussion among the students. To post a message to the list, send an e-mail to the Listserv address that you received in your welcome message. You may choose to discuss a current class topic. The discussion can be conducted in class, or it can be assigned as homework.

Assign one student per week to lead a discussion topic on the Listserv. The student is in charge of posting an initial question and monitoring the discussion.

Encourage students in your foreign language class to join an existing Listserv in the field of foreign language studies. They can pick an area they are interested in, such as culture, learning strategies, and so on.

Ask your students to follow up on the discussions not only reading others' postings on the Listserv but also by raising questions and responding to others.

Have students report on their Listserv discussion experience occasionally in class, focusing on what they have learned in their area of interest.

Tricks and Traps

- ◆ **Trap:** There is an abundance of free and already existing Listserv software available to teachers and students. How do you select the most appropriate Listserv?

  - • **Trick:** If you plan to encourage your students to subscribe to public Listservs, it is a good idea to monitor or check the archives of the Listserv before asking your students to join. You'll also want to make sure that the list is active. Often, Listservs are created but not used. You can sometimes check the archives to see how active a Listserv is.

- ◆ **Trap:** There are several addresses associated with each Listserv. How do you know which address to use?

- **Trick:** It is a good idea to keep the welcome message that you receive when you set up a Listserv. This message contains several important e-mail addresses. It contains the address used to subscribe and unsubscribe to the Listserv, as well as the address used to post a message to all the members of the Listserv. If you keep the welcome message, you will have easy access to all the crucial addresses to the Listserv and will be able to perform these functions.

- **Trap:** You go on vacation and cannot check your e-mail while you are away. When you return, your mailbox is full of messages. What can you do?

  - **Trick:** The welcome message you receive will contain all the details of unsubscribing to the list. If you plan to go on vacation or will not be able to check your e-mail for several days, you may want to consider unsubscribing to the Listserv. Once you return from vacation, you can easily subscribe to the Listserv again.

- **Trap:** The Listserv is very active, and you receive several e-mail messages a day from the Listserv.

  - **Trick:** Many Listservs provide the option to receive all the e-mails as they are posted to the Listserv or to receive a digest. A digest is one e-mail per day that includes all the messages from that day. If you are receiving too many e-mails from the Listserv, it may be beneficial to sign up to receive a digest of the e-mails.

Reflections

- How can I use Listservs to encourage participation from all students?

- How can I use Listservs to promote productive skills?

- How can I use Listservs to discuss culture?

- How can I use Listservs to access culture?

- How can I use Listservs to access native speakers?

Enjoy!

Activity 1: Complete a Poem

- Nature of the activity: Creative collaborative work.

- Type of activity: This is a whole-class activity. The goal is for students to be creative with the target language.

- Proficiency level: Advanced beginning to advanced fluency.

- Time: This activity can be done in class or as a homework assignment. If it is done in class, it will take approximately 30 minutes. If it is done as a homework assignment, it can last much longer, depending on how often the students participate.

- Skills: Reading and writing in the target language.

- Additional materials: Dictionary.

The teacher selects a poem and posts the first few lines of the poem on the Listserv. Ask students to predict the following lines of the poem.

Standards met in this activity...	
ACTFL Standards	ISTE NETS Standards
1.1, 1.2, 3.1	II-C, II-D, III-C

Activity 2: Join a discussion of French culture in the United States

- Nature of the activity: Collaborative or individual.

- Type of activity: This can be a whole-class activity or an individual activity.

- Proficiency level: Advanced beginning to advanced fluency.

- Time: This activity can be done in class or as a homework assignment. The time is variable because you can ask students to participate for the entire school year, one month, or one week.

- Skills: Reading and writing in the target language.

- Additional materials: Dictionary.

You and your students join the "French Culture in the U.S." Listserv. Go to http://www.frenchculture.org/newsletter/subscribe.asp to subscribe to the Listserv. Read and participate in the discussion as long you desire. Report to the class on what you found interesting in the discussion and discuss the Listserv topics in class.

Standards met in this activity...	
ACTFL Standards	ISTE NETS Standards
2.1, 2.2	II-C, II-D, V-C

Activity 3: Proverbs

- ♦ Nature of the activity: Creative collaborative work.

- ♦ Type of activity: This is a whole-class activity.

- ♦ Proficiency level: Advanced beginning to advanced fluency.

- ♦ Time: This activity can be done in class or as a homework assignment. If it is done in class, it will take approximately 15 minutes. If it is done as a homework assignment, it can last much longer, depending on how often the students participate.

- ♦ Skills: Reading and writing in the target language.

- ♦ Additional materials: Dictionary.

The teacher or an assigned student posts a proverb in the target language on the class Listserv. Students read the proverb and post their understanding of the proverb. Students respond to one another's postings.

Standards met in this activity...	
ACTFL Standards	**ISTE NETS Standards**
1.1, 1.2, 2.1, 2.2	II-D, III-B, III-C

Activity 4: Riddles

- ♦ Nature of the activity: Creative collaborative work.

- ♦ Type of activity: This is a whole-class activity.

- ♦ Proficiency level: Advanced beginning to advanced fluency.

- ♦ Time: This activity can be done in class or as a homework assignment. If it is done in class, it will take approximately 15 minutes. If it is done as a homework assignment, it can last much longer, depending on how often the students participate.

- ♦ Skills: Reading and writing in the target language.

- ♦ Additional materials: Dictionary.

The teacher or an assigned student posts a riddle or a mystery in the target language on the class Listserv. Students read the riddle or mystery and post their answers on the Listserv. Students respond to one another's postings.

Standards met in this activity...	
ACTFL Standards	**ISTE NETS Standards**
1.1, 1.2	II-D, III-B, III-C

Activity 5: Interview Native Speakers

♦ Nature of the activity: Individual, pair, or group work.

♦ Type of activity: This is individual, pair, or group activity.

♦ Proficiency level: Advanced beginning to advanced fluency.

♦ Time: This activity can be done in class or as a homework assignment. If it is done in class, it will take approximately 30 minutes. If it is done as a homework assignment, it can last much longer, depending on how often the students participate.

♦ Skills: Reading and writing in the target language.

♦ Additional materials: Dictionary.

Students join an established Listserv with native speakers of the target language. Students write up interview questions individually, in pairs, or as a group. Students post their interview questions on the discussion board. Students interact with native speakers as they receive responses.

Standards met in this activity...	
ACTFL Standards	**ISTE NETS Standards**
1.1, 1.2, 2.1, 2.2, 5.1	II-D, III-C, V-C

10

Internet Chat: Yahoo! Messenger and Chat

Sha Balizet

My class really likes chatting online. We often use chat at the end of an activity, so students can debrief it. It's a great way to exchange opinions, and I think it helps their fluency.

Eleventh-grade Spanish teacher

Chat and Instant Messaging in the Foreign Language Classroom

Real-time communication software (also known as "chat") lets you communicate electronically. It is like a phone call in that it is instantaneous communication, but it does not occur face to face. Chat interaction typically takes place in text mode as you type on a computer to communicate with another person. Chat is like a telephone conversation because it is immediate. You do not have a delay in communication, as you do with e-mail and other forms of asynchronous communication. Chat lets you interact with an individual or a group; you can interact with friends or students or meet new people around the world.

Because chat communication takes place with no time lag, it is particularly helpful for developing students' fluency and rate of language production. Chat can be used for any activity in which you might otherwise use face-to-face communication in pairs or small groups. With chat, however, shy students can "speak up," whereas they might not do so in face-to-face interaction. Chat also helps build written-language skill development.

To use chat with your students, you will need computers with an Internet connection and browser software to view Web pages. Many Web sites offer free chat. This chapter will guide you through the process of registering for and using Yahoo! software for chatting and instant messaging.

Just try this!

First you will set up an identity on the Yahoo! Web site, then download Yahoo! Messenger chat software. This software allows you to chat online, exchanging instant messages in chat rooms. You can chat with others who are on the Yahoo! chat site, either in one-on-one conversations or as part of a group chat. If you have a Windows computer, you can chat in text or voice mode. Only text-based chat is available for Macintosh users.

The Yahoo! Messenger system has chat rooms in which you can interact in English, French, German, Italian, Spanish, and Asian languages.

Learn to Use Yahoo! Messenger

Step 1   Go to the Yahoo! Web site

♦ You can go straight to the chat site by typing this address in your browser's address box: http://chat.yahoo.com. Then hit **Enter**, and the browser will open the Yahoo! chat page.

Step 2   Register to become a Yahoo! member

♦ Register with Yahoo! so that you can use its services. On the main Yahoo! chat page, click on **Sign Up for Yahoo! Chat!** and fill out the registration form.

♦ Set up your preferred content. This is a great feature for language teachers. "Localizing" Yahoo! means that you can view Yahoo! pages in the language of your choice and in a context of interest to you. For example, you can set up your Yahoo! account to display Chinese language in the context of the United States, China, Singapore, or Hong Kong.

♦ Select a Yahoo! identity. This ID will be your online name. Protect your privacy by choosing an ID that is not your real name. Be aware that many people use Yahoo!, and your nickname might already be taken. You might need to make your nickname unique by adding numbers, for example.

♦ Set up your password question and answer and an alternate e-mail address. This is important in case you forget your Yahoo! password. (A good security practice is to use different passwords. Do not write down your password!)

♦ At the bottom of the form you will find the End User License Agreement. Read this carefully. To use the Yahoo! services, you must click on the **Accept** button to indicate that you accept the agreement.

♦ When your registration is complete, you can move on to the next step.

Step 3   Download and install the Yahoo! Messenger software

◆ On the main Yahoo! chat page, http://chat.yahoo.com, go to the section called **My Chat** in the middle of the page.

◆ Click on the link that reads **Get Yahoo! Messenger to stay in touch with your friends**.

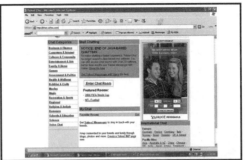

◆ A pop-up menu will give you an overview of the download procedure.

◆ The Yahoo! software will detect your computer's operating system (Windows 98, XP, or Vista, for example) and offer you the best software for your system. (The example in this guide follows the procedure for a computer running Windows 95, 98, NT, or 2000 and Internet Explorer 3.0 or higher. For other systems or software, the procedure is similar.)

◆ Yahoo! Messenger will automatically begin downloading the installation wizard.

◆ The Yahoo! Messenger installation wizard will load to your computer, and then you will see a Welcome! pop-up window. Begin the software installation by clicking the **Next** button.

◆ Choose the version of Yahoo! Messenger that you want to install. The basic installation is Yahoo! Messenger only, which requires about 5 megabytes (MB) of space on your computer.

◆ Select where you want the software to be located on your computer. You can click **OK** to accept the automatic selection or choose **Browse** to change the file location.

◆ Read the License Agreement and click the check box next to **Yes, I accept the terms of this agreement**.

◆ Click **Next** to continue.

◆ A **Ready to Install!** window appears. You will see the approximate time needed to download the software to your computer. Click **Next** to continue, then wait as the software installs.

◆ Yahoo! Messenger will notify you of the installation results when the process is complete. If you experience any problems with the software installation, go online to Yahoo! Chat Help.

◆ Make sure that the box next to **Launch Yahoo! Messenger** is checked.

◆ Click **Finish**.

Congratulations! You have installed Yahoo! Messenger software on your computer!

Step 4 Log in and connect to the Yahoo! instant messaging system

- Type in the Yahoo! ID and password that you created in Step 2.

- Warning: Practice good security habits. If you share a computer or use a computer lab, do not check the box next to **Remember my ID and password** when you log in.

- Click the **Login** button.

Step 5 Find friends online and add friends to your Yahoo! Messenger address book

- Search for your friends' Yahoo! IDs. If you don't know a student's or friend's Yahoo! ID, you might be able to locate it. Go to http://members.yahoo.com/ and search from this page.

  (*Note:* This search only works if your contact has entered his or her information and has reported it honestly.)

- Add people to your Yahoo! contact list.

- Now that you have your friends' Yahoo! IDs, you can list them in your online address book.

- To add a person to your contacts list, just click the **Contacts** menu, then select **Add a Contact**. A popup menu will appear. Fill in your friend's Yahoo! ID or e-mail address. The wizard will help you complete the entry.

Now you are getting it!

Step 6 Practice chatting with a friend or colleague

- Show a friend or colleague how to sign up for Yahoo! Messenger. Give your friend your Yahoo! ID and have your friend add you to his or her contacts list (contacts must mutually agree to be one another's lists).

- To add a contact to your Messenger contacts list, first send a request to your friend.

- The friend will receive a **New Contact Request**. He or she has a choice of approving or denying the request.

- When you receive a **New Contact Request** from a friend, the most convenient response is to click **Allow and Add to My Messenger List**. Choosing this option lets you add friends to your list easily.

- Be very cautious in adding strangers to your list.

Step 7   Send a Yahoo! message to your friend

- Double-click on the name of your friend. A **Message** window will pop up. (*Note:* If you position your cursor over the name of a friend, a pop-up window will appear. From this window, you can select from several options—chat, computer-to-computer call, text message, e-mail.)

- Type your message in the box at the bottom of the screen.

- To send the message, click **Send** or hit the **Enter** key.

- You will see a pop-up window telling you that your message has been sent.

- Your message will now appear in the top window.

- Your friend will receive your message immediately if he or she is online. If your friend is offline, he or she will receive your message the next time he or she logs in to Yahoo! Messenger.

Step 8   Receive and reply to a Yahoo! message

- Replying to a message is even easier than sending a new one!

- When you receive a message, simply click the **Reply** button and type your message. Click the **Send** button to deliver your reply.

- You may not want to answer a message from a stranger. In that case, click **Delete** to erase the stranger's message. Click **Ignore** to refuse all messages from a sender.

Step 9   Use Yahoo! Messenger to encourage students' language learning

- Practice using Yahoo! Messenger with a friend until you are comfortable with the basic mechanics of the software.

- Next, teach your students how to use Yahoo! Messenger.

- Use the target language as you take them through the process outlined here. This way, teaching about technology helps support authentic communication in the target language. Even students who know about chat will find much to learn!

♦ Next, give students a small assignment to help them—and you!—become more familiar with chat. For example, have them ask each other questions using new vocabulary.

You have got something to smile about!

Learn to Use Instant Communication With Others in a Chat Room Environment

Step 10　Find and enter a chat room

♦ You can enter a chat room and talk to a group of people. Go to the Yahoo! Messenger menu (at the top of the Yahoo! screen) and choose **Yahoo! Chat > Join a Room**.

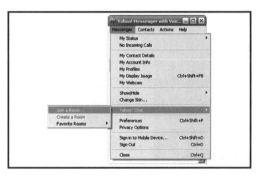

♦ There are many rooms to choose from in the **Join a Group** window. One place to start is the Yahoo! category called **Cultures and Community**. You can join a chat with native speakers of the target language.

Warning: Use good sense and caution in your behavior online. Online and chat environments might not be appropriate for all users.

♦ Click the **+** symbol to the left of **Cultures and Community**.

♦ Click **By Language** and select the language group in the pane on the right.

♦ Expand a selection by clicking on **+**.

♦ Click on the name of the chat room you wish to join, then click **Go to Room** to enter that room.

Step 11   Talk in a chat room

- You can wait and watch the group conversation unfold. You do not have to participate.

- If you want to chat with everyone in the room, type in the box at the bottom of the screen, then hit the **Enter** key.

- You can talk to an individual privately inside a chat room. To send an instant message to one person, click the user's name. An **Instant Message** window will appear.

- Use caution and good sense when interacting in chat rooms. Be forewarned that chat can be graphic and offensive.

Step 12   Set up a private chat room for your class

- In a private chat room, you and your students can "speak" to the whole class instantaneously in chat mode. Your private chat room is secure from unwelcome outsiders.

- Create your own room using the Yahoo! Messenger menu (at the top of the Yahoo! screen) by selecting **Yahoo! Chat > Create a Room**.

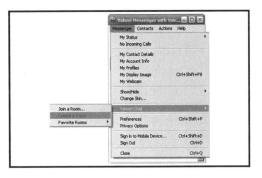

Step 13   Identify your chat room

- Choose a category for your chat room (e.g., Cultures or Education).

- Name your chat room.

- Write a welcome message.

- Select the level of access. Use good sense and restrict access to your students and authorized guests. Select **Private** so that users may join the room only if they are invited them.

- You might also want to enable voice messaging if your computers are equipped with headsets or with microphones and speakers.

- Click on **Open Room**. This window will disappear.

Step 14   Complete the set up and enter your private chat room

- Click the **Go to Room** button.

- Using Yahoo! Messenger, send invitations to your students to join you in the private chat room.

- Hold a class discussion!

Tricks and Traps

- **Trap:** Online chatters can be sexually offensive and sometimes dangerous.

  - **Trick:** Use caution in your online behavior! In chat rooms, avoid public rooms for class activities. Use only private chat rooms with your students. Restrict access to class members and visitors whom you authorize.

- **Trap:** Students can be distracted from real class work when they have access to Yahoo! Messenger.

  - **Trick:** Keep your students busy—so busy with class activities using chat that they have no time for distractions. Make your students accountable for producing work in the target language during class to help them focus on learning.

- **Another Trick:** Use chat as an incentive! Allow students to chat—in the target language, of course!—as a reward for learning.

Reflections

- Are my students using the technology to learn effectively, or are conversations shallow and pointless? Have I planned activities so that students are given specific topics and purposes?

- Have I set my objectives and assessments appropriately for the medium? Have I kept in mind that instant messaging is real-time communication? This mode is good for developing fluency but less helpful for focusing on accuracy. How have I worked with the strengths of this medium in my lesson and evaluation?

- Have I considered the impact of grouping and ability in planning activities? Have I expected more participation in smaller groups and less in larger ones, as in face-to-face communications? Have I recognized the advantages of fast typists and computer-savvy students?

- Have I considered grouping students into mixed-ability pairs? Have I tried to increase language use by assigning one student to dictate and the partner to listen and type?

- Is my assessment in keeping with my lesson? Am I using chat for assessment when I use it for instruction? Or am I using paper-and-pencil assessments to measure the students' learning through chat? How can I improve the quality of my assessment so that I can make sound educational decisions?

- Have I followed safe, secure computing practices? Have I used a privacy-protecting nickname for online interactions? Do I require the same of my students? Do I ensure that my students are safe from online predators by using private chat rooms? If I am using a Web-based chat service, have I investigated them? Are privacy and security policies strict enough to protect my students? Remembering that viruses can be spread through electronic attachments, have I chosen to restrict or allow attachments? Do my students and I use a virus protection software program?

- Have I kept a log or journal of my chat experiences? Have I jotted down the different activities, student groupings, and outcomes? Have I noted the positive benefits of the chat experience, ways to improve or change, and any technical problems?

- Have I helped other teachers learn to use chat with their students?

Enjoy!

Activity 1: Reading Chat

- Nature of the activity: Online discussion of a text.

- Type of activity: This is a small-group activity that requires students to share their understanding of a text read prior to the activity.

- Proficiency level: Advanced beginning to advanced fluency.

- Time: 10–40 minutes (depending on the complexity of the text).

- Skills: Reading and writing skills in the target language.

- Additional materials: Proficiency-level and age-appropriate text to be read prior the discussion.

Assign students a reading and a task based on the reading that is appropriate to the students' proficiency level. For example, lower-level students could be assigned to discuss vocabulary or structure, whereas higher-level classes might be ready to examine the writer's tone or style. Divide the class into groups of three or four. Set up several private chat rooms, one for each group and one for the whole class. Designate one student in each group to act as the leader. The leader will facilitate the discussion, making sure every group member contributes. Assign another student to act as the reporter, summarizing the discussion. Give students a time limit for their discussion.

Connect to the Internet and log on to Yahoo! Messenger (if the program does not start automatically). The leader should send a message to all of the members in his or her group to start off the discussion. At the end of the discussion, each group should print a transcript of their discussion and summary and turn it in to you. Evaluate students' participation and fluency, as well as their task effectiveness. To help them improve, report the evaluation results to your students. To help you improve, reflect on this chat lesson. Evaluate what worked well and what needed improvement.

Standards met in this activity...	
ACTFL Standards	ISTE NETS Standards
1.1, 1.2, 1.3, 2.1, 2.2, 3.2, 5.1	I-A, I-B, II-A, II-E, III-A, III-B, III-C, III-D, IV-A, IV-B, IV-C, V-B

Activity 2: Messenger-Pair Study

♦ Nature of the activity: Collaborative review

♦ Type of activity: This is a dyad activity in which students support each other while checking their homework or reviewing material.

♦ Proficiency level: Intermediate to advanced fluency.

♦ Time: 20–30 minutes (depending on the complexity of the task).

♦ Skills: Reading and writing skills in the target language.

♦ Additional materials: Textbook and class material.

Divide students into pairs. Using Yahoo! Messenger, have students check their homework with their partner. You could also use this for review before a test. Permit students to instant message you or a class leader if they are unable to answer particular questions. You could also require student self-assessment at the end of the study period. This helps students stay focused and develop metacognitive awareness.

Standards met in this activity...	
ACTFL Standards	ISTE NETS Standards
1.1, 1.2, 1.3, 3.2, 5.1	I-B, II-A, II-E, III-A, III-B, III-C, III-D, V-A, V-B, V-C

Activity 3: Role Play

- ◆ Nature of the activity: Role play

- ◆ Type of activity: This is a dyad activity in which students support each other while checking their homework or reviewing material.

- ◆ Proficiency level: Advanced beginners to advanced fluency.

- ◆ Time: 10–30 minutes (depending on the complexity of the scenario).

- ◆ Skills: Reading and writing skills in the target language.

- ◆ Additional materials: Play scenario.

Almost any role play that you do in a face-to-face setting can be conducted through online chat. Little adaptation is needed other than the technology. Online chat role play builds spontaneity and ease in second language speech and improves vocabulary, grammar, spelling, and reading. Students enjoy chat—even shy students. You can expect participation in role play in instant message mode—with the benefit of blissful quiet for you, even when every student is chatting online! Another advantage of chat is the ability to print out all of the conversation. This printout can help you diagnose students' strengths and weaknesses; you and your students can build on this foundation in future classes.

Standards met in this activity...	
ACTFL Standards	**ISTE NETS Standards**
1.1, 1.2, 1.3, 2.1, 2.2, 3.2, 5.1	I-B, II-A, II-E, III-A, III-B, III-C, III-D, IV-A, IV-B, IV-C, V-B

Activity 4: Explore and Report!

- ◆ Nature of the activity: Individual online exploration with follow-up report in a chat room.

- ◆ Type of activity: This is an individual activity that involves reading in the target language and reporting to the class.

- ◆ Proficiency level: Advanced beginners to advanced fluency.

- ◆ Time: 20–30 minutes (depending on the complexity of the online reading).

- ◆ Skills: Reading and writing skills in the target language.

- ◆ Additional materials: Web sites in the target language.

Assign individuals to investigate a target language Web site. Students should take note of important features on the site. You might assign them to explore the use of vocabulary, for example, or grammatical features; you might ask them to search for cultural features on the site. Do not use a single Web site for the whole class, as the connections will be very slow. Instead, find four or five different sites and distribute the site assignments within a group. At the end of the exploration period (however long you wish that to be), students should report on the results of their investigations. Ask individuals to report back to a small group or the whole class. You can give students a prompt sheet to help guide students' answers.

You also can use a rubric or checklist to measure student outcomes according to the unit objectives. The following factors might be learned or developed in a foreign language lesson: language skills, language fluency, cultural knowledge, cultural appreciation, subject-area knowledge, summarizing skills, presentation skills, analytical skills, and evaluation skills. Measure the skills and information that are important in your lesson so that you and your students will know how well they have learned.

Standards met in this activity...	
ACTFL Standards	ISTE NETS Standards
1.1, 1.2, 1.3, 2.1, 2.2, 3.2, 5.1	I-B, II-A, E, III-A, B, C, D, IV-A, B, C, V-B

Activity 5: Chat Room Interview of Special Guest

♦ Nature of the activity: Group discussion.

♦ Type of activity: This activity may be a small-group or a class activity, depending on the number of native-speaking guests you invite to participate. This activity involves online conversation on a topics related to the target culture (suggested grammar point: interrogative sentences).

♦ Proficiency level: Advanced beginners to advanced fluency.

♦ Time: 20–30 minutes (depending on the size of the group).

♦ Skills: Speaking, reading, and writing skills in the target language.

♦ Additional materials: None.

Bringing a native-speaking guest to your class has never been so easy! In fact, your guest does not even need to leave home—all the visitor needs is chat software and authorization to enter your private chat room.

For optimal learning, structure the event so that students prepare before the chat. Students might prepare by researching the guest's home country, culture, or area of expertise. Students should brainstorm questions to ask the guest. Require older or more advanced students to anticipate the guest's answer to questions and plan follow-up questions.

Consider the outcomes that you expect from this activity and plan your assessment accordingly. For example, this unit could lead students to learn about the target culture or country, as well as develop their language knowledge and use. Cover all of the dimensions involved in the learning event for best measurement.

Standards met in this activity...	
ACTFL Standards	**ISTE NETS Standards**
1.1, 1.2, 1.3, 2.1, 2.2, 5.1, 5.2	I-B, III-C, III-D, IV-C, IV-D, V-D

11

New Audio: Voice Over Internet Protocol Services

Zhaohui Chen and Deborah Cordier

When we do individual work stations, I have my students talk to people from all over the world, ...well at least to people from many different Spanish-speaking countries. They and the callee get a big kick out of it.

Eleventh-grade Spanish teacher

About Voice Over Internet Protocol Services

New technologies based on the basic principles of telephone service are being used to communicate over the Internet. With a computer, an Internet connection, and a few simple steps, foreign language speakers and learners can connect with and call one another across time zones.

Skype (http://www.skype.com) and Gizmo (http://www.gizmoproject.com) are two of the most popular services, and they are currently available free. Voice over Internet Protocol (VoIP) work in the same way that a phone line carries your voice, but your voice is instead carried over the Internet. With Skype, you can dial a contact, and, provided the person you are calling has also downloaded Skype, you can talk to and from any country, using a headset and microphone plugged into your computer.

There is no charge to call anywhere in the world, and you can speak any foreign language together, as long as both you and the person you are calling have Internet access and Skype installed on your computers. Gizmo works like Skype and must be downloaded and installed.

Just try this!

Step 1

♦ To use Skype for the first time, visit Skype's Web site, http://www.skype.com. The default page is in English. From the top of the page, you can select a different language using the **Change** option. Select your language from the choices provided.

Step 2

♦ Download the Skype software to your computer. Click on **Download** and choose the appropriate version Skype for your operating system (Windows, Mac Os X, Linux, or Pocket PC).

Step 3

♦ The set-up wizard will take you step-by-step through the installation process. Skype's features offer a variety of ways to practice your foreign language skills with your teacher or other learners. You can talk to one person or to multiple people simultaneously, you can participate in a video call, you can share files, or you can do text chat.

Now you are getting it!

Communicating With Audio

Step 4

♦ If your contact is online, click the green phone button to dial. If you cannot find your contact, you will need to invite him or her to join Skype. Users must sign up with Skype and choose a User ID. When you know your contact's User ID, add him or her to your Skype contacts. To do this, go to the **Add Contact** button on the menu bar. Search for your contact's User ID and add the contact to your list. It is as simple as A, B, C!

Step 5

Call your contact by clicking on the green call button

Step 6

♦ Now speak together, making sure you have appropriate speakers and a microphone.

Communicating With Chat and Sharing Files

Step 7

♦ With Skype, you can also chat online. Locate your contact as you did before, then click on the **Chat** button on the upper right-hand side of your communication window.

Step 8

♦ You can send files to your contacts by clicking on the **Send File** button on the upper right-hand side of your communication window. If the button is not displayed, you will need to click on the double right-hand arrow to access it or maximize the Skype communication window.

You have got something to smile about!

Use Skype to set up a conversation lesson with a foreign language student. Remember, the students must have an Internet connection and must install Skype on his or her computer before you can begin.

Don't forget about Skype's conferencing function. At the top menu of the communication window, choose **Conference**. A pop-up window will appear, with your contacts listed on the left-hand side. Using the **Add** and **Remove** buttons, arrange your Skype conference and get ready for a small-group activity in the target language.

Tricks and Traps

♦ **Trap:** You Are Experiencing Technical Problems with Skype. For example: you cannot hear your partner, the computers you have at school are behind a restricted firewall, or you are not sure how much bandwidth Skype uses.

• **Trick:** Skype is very user friendly, and the creators have developed a detailed set of Frequently Asked Questions that will provide you with all of your technical solutions.

♦ **Trap:** Your contacts can see you online during a call and interrupt you while you are on a call. What do you do? Are you trapped?

• **Trick:** Right-click on the Skype icon on the bottom taskbar and choose **Change Status**. On the **Status** drop-down menu, choose the status that best meets your needs.

♦ **Trap:** You have had many voice and chat sessions on Skype but did not track them: You don't remember who initiated them, how long they were, or on what dates they occurred. What do you do? Are you trapped?

• **Trick:** In your communication window, find the **History** tab. When you click on it, you will see the list of all your communication activities. Information about type of activity, date, time, and duration is provided. You can revisit the text chat and access the files your contacts have sent you.

Reflections

♦ What steps should I follow to set up pen pals for my students using Skype?

♦ How could I use Skype to converse with a student living in a foreign country?

♦ How could I include discussion in a Skype session?

♦ What strategies could be employed to make distance communication more effective and encourage students to stay on-task during communication?

Activity 1: Pair-Up

♦ Nature of the activity: Collaborative work.

♦ Type of activity: This is a pair activity that encourages collaboration between students through the discussion of assigned topics using Skype. The goal is to engage students in using the target language in oral or written discussion.

♦ Proficiency level: Advanced beginners and higher.

♦ Time: The activity can be conducted in various lengths or as a supplement to other class content. It can also be conducted as after-class collaboration among students in pairs.

♦ Skills: Speaking and writing.

In the computer lab, the teacher divides students into pairs. Each pair is assigned a different topic, such as a cultural aspect of the target language. Students in each pair work from their own computer using Skype. Students can use either audio/video or chat in their discussion.

Standards met in this activity...	
ACTFL Standards	ISTE NETS Standards
1.1, 1.3, 3.2, 5.1	I-A, I-D, II-B, II-D

Activity 2: Let's Do a Project Together

♦ Nature of the activity: Collaborative work.

♦ Type of activity: This is a group activity that requires students to work in small groups on a project.

♦ Proficiency level: Intermediate to advanced fluency.

♦ Time: This activity can be done in stages, depending on the actual working process in each group.

♦ Skills: Speaking, reading, and writing skills in the target language.

The teacher divides students into groups of three or four. The activity can be conducted in the computer lab, as a homework assignment, or as a combination of the two. Each group is assigned a topic to work on, and they should discuss the procedures for the project and the roles of each group member. Each member of the group works on his or her own computer but collaborates with other group members through Skype's data transfer features. If necessary, groups can engage in audio or chat communication using Skype. After the project is done, each group shares their project with the whole class.

Standards met in this activity...	
ACTFL Standards	ISTE NETS Standards
1.1, 1.3, 3.2, 5.1	I-A, I-D, II-B, II-D

Activity 3: Online Pen Pals

- ◆ Nature of the activity: Collaborative work between students and native speakers of the target language.

- ◆ Type of activity: This activity allows students to collaborate with native speakers of the target language. The goal is to engage students in real communication (through audio, video, chat, etc.) in the target language.

- ◆ Proficiency level: Intermediate to advanced fluency.

- ◆ Time: Variable.

- ◆ Skills: Speaking, reading, and writing skills in the target language.

The teacher helps students to set up contact with pen pals (ideally, native speakers of the target language, but the pen pals could be also target language students from a different school). Each student has a pen pal. A convenient time is set up for both students and the pen pals. During that time, each student uses Skype to communicate with his or her pen pal. Students can present their pen pals to the class later in the semester.

Suggestion: The students and pen pals should choose a specific topic(s) that they will discuss. A list of topics can be provided by the teacher.

Standards met in this activity...	
ACTFL Standards	ISTE NETS Standards
1.1, 1.3, 3.2, 5.1	I-A, I-D, II-B, II-D

Activity 4: Let's Do Video Conferencing

- ◆ Nature of the activity: Collaborative work between students and native speakers of the target language.

- ◆ Type of activity: This activity allows students to collaborate with native speakers of the target language.

- ◆ Proficiency level: Intermediate to advanced fluency.

- Time: Variable.

- Skills: Speaking skills in the target language.

Contact a school in a country where the target language is spoken. Arrange a video conferencing session.

It is best to conduct the video conference with a small size class (five to six students) so that everyone has an opportunity to participate in the video conference. If it is difficult to find a school in another country or the time difference is insurmountable, try to find a local immersion school where the target language is taught. The video conference will start automatically if a camera is plugged into the computer.

Standards met in this activity...	
ACTFL Standards	ISTE NETS Standards
1.1, 1.3, 3.2, 5.1	I-A, I-D, II-B, II-D

Activity 5: Homework Is Fun

- Nature of the activity: Collaborative work between students.

- Type of activity: This activity allows students to collaborate with their classmates to communicate in the target language for a specific purpose.

- Proficiency level: Intermediate to advanced fluency.

- Time: Variable.

- Skills: Speaking, reading, and writing skills in the target language.

The teacher gives a homework assignment to the students. If students have a computer at home and Internet access, they can communicate with other classmates using Skype to discuss the homework, collaborate on the homework, solve problems together, and share resources.

Standards met in this activity...	
ACTFL Standards	ISTE NETS Standards
1.1, 1.3, 3.2, 5.1	I-A, I-D, II-B, II-D

Activity 6: Conduct Conversation Lessons Using Skype

- Nature of the activity: Practice speaking in a foreign language.

- Type of activity: This activity allows students to communicate in the target language for a specific purpose and encourages teacher–student interaction.

- Proficiency level: Beginner to advanced fluency.

- Time: Approximately one hour.

- Skills: Speaking skills in the target language.

The teacher assigns a lesson by e-mail. Students arrange to contact the teacher at a specified time to conduct the lesson using Skype. The teacher and the student can talk and support their oral communication with written messages (text chat) and file exchange.

Standards met in this activity...	
ACTFL Standards	ISTE NETS Standards
1.1, 1.3, 3.2, 5.1	I-A, I-D, II-B, II-D

Activity 7: Online Foreign Language Video

- Nature of the activity: Discussion of an assigned foreign language video viewed prior to the Skype session.

- Type of activity: Encourage oral and listening skills in the discussion of assigned topics using Skype. The goal is to engage students in oral or written discussion in the target language using conversation or chat through Skype.

- Proficiency level: Intermediate to advance.

- Time: The activity can be conducted in various lengths or as a supplement to lesson content.

- Skills: Speaking and writing.

The teacher assigns students to watch a foreign language video and distributes questions for review and preparation by e-mail or chat. Students work from their own computers. Students can use either an audio/video connection or chat in their discussion through Skype. The activity is best assigned as a small-group activity (using conferencing) so that the teacher can monitor and participate in the communication.

Standards met in this activity...	
ACTFL Standards	ISTE NETS Standards
1.1, 1.3, 3.2, 5.1	I-A, I-D, II-B, II-D

Section IV

E-Extensions

12

The Nice of Nicenet: Web-Based Tools for Managing the Foreign Language Classroom

Iona Sarieva and Annmarie Zoran

Before Nicenet I had all these pieces of paper, which I and my students were always losing. Now with Nicenet all the class material is in one place and it is always available to me and my students even after the course is over.

ESL instructor

About Nicenet

Internet Classroom Assistant 2 (ICA2), commonly known as Nicenet (http://nicenet.org), is a courseware management application developed by Nicenet—a volunteer nonprofit organization dedicated to providing free services to the Internet community. Nicenet serves the same purpose as Blackboard or WebCT. The application is free of charge and contains no advertising, It is designed for a variety of educational settings from elementary to post-secondary. The uncomplicated design makes the application easy to adopt and use. The only requirement of Nicenet is an Internet connection; no additional software needs to be installed, and the application functions on any Web browser. Nicenet's creators promote it as a highly intuitive application that requires no formal training. They point out that the low graphic content of the interface makes it easy to use with a lower-speed connection. Once an instructor creates a virtual class, it is available at any time and can be modified, edited, and shaped according to the class needs.

Just try this!

Nicenet is a wonderful way to manage and administrate your classroom: It allows instructors to create online portfolios, classroom discussion lists, and shared Web link collections and provide online access to class calendars and homework assignments. In other words, it acts as a course management tool.

To get started on any computer, Mac or PC, follow these steps:

Step 1

◆ Open your Internet browser.

Step 2

◆ Go to http://www.nicenet.org. Congratulations! You are on the Nicenet login page. Now you can create your class or join an already established class.

◆ From the login page, click on **Join a Class**.

◆ On the next page, you will see **Step 1: Enter the class key**. Enter the class key that is provided by the class instructor. For this activity, enter class key 248674S98 (conference page).

◆ Click on **Join the Class**.

◆ Fill out the information on the registration page. (*Hint:* Use an e-mail account that you access frequently.)

◆ Click on **Join the Class**.

◆ Read the Nicenet terms of agreement and regulations and click **Finish Registration**.

◆ Type in your username and password. (*Hint:* Your username must be unique; to make it unique and easy to remember, you might use your first name and the last two digits of your home phone number.)

◆ Click on **Log in to the ICA**.

◆ Congratulations! You successfully logged in to the Nicenet Intro Class. You can browse the class to learn how to work with Nicenet and continue with the book.

♦ After you have entered your class key, you do not need to keep it anymore; however, you must remember your username and password.

Welcome to the "CALLing All Foreign Language Teachers" Nicenet Class

Here, we have posted information that will make it easier for you to understand how Nicenet is organized. We hope that you will also participate in our online discussions, hosted in the Conference section. You can also view the Link Sharing section and access some of the Web sites we find useful in the foreign language classroom. You can read or post your own documents in the Document section, view the class schedule posted by the instructor, or view the list of class members.

Let's Create Your Own Class! Option A

This section is for those of you who joined our "CALLing All Foreign Language Teachers" course. If you skipped the section called "Join a Nicenet Class" and have never created a Nicenet account, please refer to the next section, "Let's Create Your Own Class! Option B"

Step 3

♦ Go to the Classes section on the left-hand navigation menu and choose **Create**.

Step 4

♦ Follow the instructions provided.

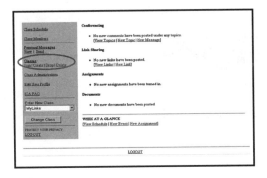

Let's Create Your Own Class! Option B

For those of you who did not join our "CALLing All Foreign Language Teachers" course and do not have a Nicenet account, follow these steps:

Step 5

♦ Go to http://www.nicenet.org and click on **Create a Class**.

Step 6

♦ Fill out the **Start a Class** form. (*Hint:* Use this form *only* if you have not created or joined a Nicenet class.)

Congratulations! You have just created your own Nicenet class! Now it is time to play.

Create and Post a Document on Nicenet

Step 7

♦ Click on the **Document** link on the left-hand navigation menu.

Step 8

♦ To post a document, simply click on **Add Document**.

Step 9

♦ Name your document.

Step 10

♦ Now you can start typing your text. When you finish, click the **Add Document** button on the bottom of the page. (A very useful hint: You can type your text in Microsoft Word and copy and paste it into the **Document Text** window.)

Step 11

♦ After you have posted your document, it will be displayed in the same format in which your students will view it.

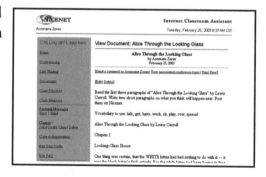

Step 12

You always have the option to edit or delete a document you have created. (Only you have these privileges—your students will not be able to alter your documents.)

♦ If you decide to print the document, you may use **Print View** option. This will give you a printer-friendly version of the text with none of the navigation menus displayed.

Now Try This

Explain to your students how to join the class that you just created. They will have to follow exactly the same steps that you did when you joined the Nicenet class. Remember, you will have to provide them with your class key. (*Hint:* If you forget your class key, don't worry. Simply go to your class home page and click on **Class Administration**. This will take you to the Class Administration page, where the class key is provided.)

Ask your students to post their next writing assignment in the Document section. For an example of a foreign language assignment, you might choose a popular children's story that is representative of the target culture. For example, for a Russian foreign language class, you might use stories by Aksakov (available on the Nicenet site).

Note: If you are using a Roman alphabet with diacritics or non-Roman alphabet, you will need to perform a few additional steps before posting your document. Refer to the step-by-step instructions in this chapter.

Do you want to promote classroom interaction? Do you think that classroom discussion ends when your students leave the class? Nicenet can help you to extend the classroom interaction between your students even after they leave school. All they will need is a computer with an Internet connection.

Now you are getting it!

How is it done? With Nicenet it is easy!

You just posted your first document in your Nicenet class. Follow these steps to create a discussion of your document:

Step 14

♦ Click on **Documents** to go to the Document section. There, you will see listed all of the documents that you have posted so far.

Step 15

♦ Choose the document for which you want to create a conference topic and click on **Edit**.

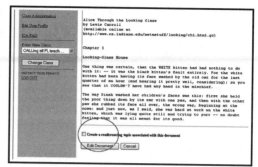

- ◆ Now you are in **Document Edit** mode. To create a conference topic, scroll down to the bottom of the page, and check box above the **Edit Document** button and click on **Edit Document**.

- ◆ Check your Conference section. You will see that there is a conference topic related to the document.

Now let's see what you and your students can do from there:

- ◆ You can post a new message under the current topic.

- ◆ You can create a new topic. (This function is accessible only to the instructor; refer to the Class Administration section for instructions.)

- ◆ You can order the messages based on the date they were posted.

- ◆ You can view only the message summaries.

- ◆ You can access the print view.

- ◆ You can answer a posted message using the **Reply** link.

- ◆ You can send a personal message to the author.

    Note: Only the author of the conference message can edit or delete it.

Now Try This

Once you have created a document and a discussion topic related to it, ask your students to share their opinions on the topic in the Conference section. You may combine this with a classroom discussion or use it as a homework assignment.

Why should you go to the trouble to incorporate online discussion into your language classroom? Here are several reasons that we found to be true of our foreign language learners:

- ◆ Students have more time to process and construct their messages. Our experience has shown that giving students an opportunity to use technology opens up interaction in a foreign language classroom: Students have more time to process the messages of their teacher and classmates and draft/edit/revise their own messages.

- ◆ Shy students like this interactive medium. Sometimes, introverted learners hesitate to share their opinions in the classroom. Nicenet provides them with the opportunity to participate in classroom discussion. In our experience, students are interested and motivated to supplement the "traditional" classroom with a more hands-on, practical approach to learning the target language.

♦ Based on surveys that were administered to students at different levels of language proficiency, we have concluded that Nicenet helps students overcome anxiety and makes them feel more comfortable participating in discussion. This suggests that computer-mediated communication lowers students' affective filter and provides a better means for authentic use of the target language.

You have got something to smile about!

Administrate Your Class!

If you choose the Class Administration view from the navigation menu, you can view all of your class information and manipulate and shape your class by

♦ Adding or deleting specific users or all users. (*Hint:* At the beginning of the school year, you may decide to reuse the same class with your new students. Simply delete last year's postings, leaving your own material, and your class is ready to go!)

♦ Changing the user type—choosing one or several students to be your assistants.

♦ Giving all users the privilege to create a conferencing topic or limiting this privilege to administrators (you) and teacher's assistants.

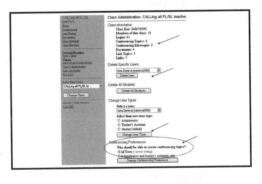

♦ In this view, you can also define your **Link Sharing** preferences, edit your class name, and choose a class to administrate if you have created multiple classes.

♦ If you can teach a language that does not use the Roman alphabet, there is some good news and some bad news for you....The bad news is that Nicenet does not allow users to directly type or copy and paste non-Roman text. The good news, however, is you can still use Nicenet. Just follow these steps:

Step 17

♦ Open a Microsoft Word document and type your text in the target language.

Step 18

♦ Click **File > Save As > Web page**. Your Word document will be saved as an HTML file.

Step 19

♦ Click **Save**. You have just created an HTML file with the same content as your Word document.

Step 20

♦ Click **View > Source** (or **HTML Source**). This will show you the codes in your document. Don't worry, you don't have to understand what is written there —just proceed to the next step.

Step 21

♦ Click **Edit > Select All**. This selects all of the code, including the content of your page.

Step 22

♦ Click **Edit > Copy**. Now your document is copied and ready to be pasted into Nicenet.

Step 23

♦ Go to your Nicenet site and log in.

Step 24

♦ Click on **Documents** and type in your subject.

Step 25

♦ Right-click in the text box and select **Paste**—you will have all the code that you copied from the Word document in the text box.

♦ Click on the **Post Document** button. Now you can view your document—you will see that all of the non-Roman characters are displayed. (*Note:* HTML tags can also be copied and pasted in Nicenet, though they are mainly used for documents and conferencing.)

Now Try This

Choose a story or text that you want to use in your classroom. Repeat Steps 1–11 to post your text on Nicenet. On our class page, we have posted an example of a Russian story by Aksakov. As you can see, all of the Cyrillic characters are there, and even more—there is a picture of a flower! We know…at the beginning of this chapter, we said that Nicenet is entirely text based. The good news is that there is a way around this problem. Refer to the instructions in this chapter to learn how to post images on Nicenet.

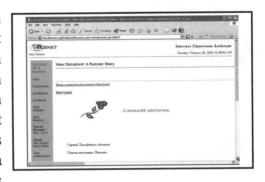

To post text with images, follow these steps. No special knowledge of HTML is required; the procedures described here involve only copying and pasting HTML tags.

Step 27

♦ Open a new Word document. Create a table and begin typing text within the table using the target language.

Step 28

♦ Choose the image you want to include in your text.

Step 29

♦ Right-click on the image and copy it. Do not close the browser; you will need to return to it one more time.

Step 30

♦ Return to the Word document. Paste the image into the document, and save the Word document as a .doc file.

Step 31

♦ Click **File > Save As > Web page**. Now you can save your Word document as an HTML file.

Step 32

♦ Click **Save**. You have just created an HTML file that has the same content as your Word document.

Step 33

♦ Go back to the online image and right-click on the image. A pop-up box will appear. Choose **Properties** and copy the address.

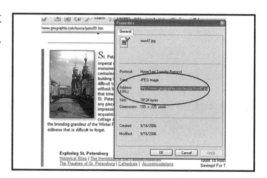

Step 34

♦ Go back to the HTML file that you created. Click **View > Source** (or **HTML Source**). This will show you the code of the document. Don't worry—you don't have to understand what is written there.

Step 35

♦ Go to **Edit > Find and Replace** and type the words **imagedata src** in the **Find Text** box. Once the text has been found, close the box.

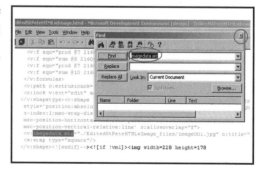

Step 36

♦ Highlight the words inside the quotation marks. (*Note:* Do not highlight the quotation marks.)

Step 37

♦ Right-click on the highlighted text and select **Paste**. This will replace the old image reference with the new online reference.

Step 38

♦ Scroll down approximately three lines and find the second place where the image is referenced.

Step 39

♦ Again, highlight everything within the quotation marks after the equal sign. Right-click and select **Paste**.

Step 40

♦ Click **Edit > Select All**. Now you have selected all of the code, including the content of your page.

Step 41

♦ Click **Edit > Copy**. Now the code is copied and ready to be pasted in Nicenet.

Step 42

♦ Go to your Nicenet site and log in.

Step 43

♦ Click on **Documents** and type in your subject.

Step 44

♦ Right-click in the text box and select **Paste**—you will have all the code that you copied from the Word document in the text box.

Step 45

♦ Click on the **Add Document** button at the bottom of the screen. Now you can view your document—you will see that all of the non-Roman characters and images are displayed.

Tricks and Traps

♦ **Trap:** Nicenet accepts only unique usernames. If your first name is Mary or your last name is Smith, you understand it will be impossible to use your own name as a username. You'll need to apply your creativity and find yourself a unique username. Keep in mind that it should be simple and easy to remember.

- **Trick:** Nicenet accepts a combination of letters and numbers as a username. Even if your name is very popular, you can still use it as a username—just add the last two or three digits of your home phone number.

♦ **Trap:** Sometimes students attempt to join a class more than once; this may create a "unique username" problem.

- **Trick:** If the student has not already registered for the class, check to see whether there is a "unique username" problem and whether the username really looks unique to you.

♦ **Trap:** Forgetting your password... It can happen to anyone.

- **Trick:** Nicenet is nice enough to provide your password to you in case you have forgotten it: A link is available on the login page. However, when registering, you must enter your e-mail address (this is an optional field in the registration form) that so Nicenet knows where to send the password.

♦ **Trap:** Nicenet does not support non-Roman characters, images, or sound files.

- **Trick:** If you use the step by step procedure outlined in this chapter, you can easily insert any non-Roman characters into your Nicenet postings.

- **Another Trick:** Don't be afraid to pick around in the HTML code! Just changing a few lines will allow you to use images in your Nicenet class. Again, you can find easy step-by-step instructions for doing this in this chapter.

- **Trick:** Although Nicenet is designed to be an asynchronous Internet communication tool, you and your students can also use it to chat. When conferencing, make sure to hit your browser's **Refresh** button so that new postings will appear.

> *Be aware—this Trick has a Trap:* Because Nicenet is designed to be used as a synchronous communication tool, there is no way to see who is currently in the Internet classroom. If you want to chat, you need to use a different means of communication to ensure the presence of your chat partner (i.e., phone, previously arranged schedule).

- **Trick:** Nicenet can also be used as a tool for communicating with parents. Parents can also log into Nicenet using the class key provided by the teacher. Parent–teacher conferences can easily be scheduled, and parents can also access class materials.

Reflections

♦ What personal characteristics are critical for successful implementation?

♦ Can Nicenet be integrated with classroom management?

♦ How do my students feel about Nicenet after using it several times?

Here is an example of a simple "Immediate Feedback" questionnaire that you can use to gauge your students' reactions:

Did you enjoy using Nicenet? Circle the face that best expresses your feelings.	
<:-0	It was confusing and frightening.
:-]	It was boring.
<:(	I don't know.
;-)	I liked it!

In Conclusion

We have found that the use of Nicenet empowers language instructors to create a constructive and effective learning environment, which, in turn, allows them to more productively meet the standards for K–12 foreign language education. These standards, developed in the 1990s by the American Council on the Teaching of Foreign Languages in collaboration with 11 professional foreign language organizations, suggest essential types of curricular experiences to enable students to achieve the standards. Acknowledging that the purposes and uses of foreign languages are as diverse as the students who study them, the standards task force identified five goal areas that embrace the following: Communication, cultures, connections, comparisons, and communities. It is within these five areas that technology can support teachers in developing instruction that meets the "5 Cs" standards. Using tools such as ICA2 can help educators develop more productive skills in these areas and provide students with opportunities to create their own virtual community and get engaged in active communication in a low-anxiety environment. Last but not least, using Web-based courseware tools, high school instructors can prepare their students for the postsecondary academic environment. Most universities in the United States are implementing Web-based courseware tools and making them a required part of the curriculum and an essential means of academic communication. Although these tools are much more complicated and incorporate a variety of functions that are not introduced in ICA2, this application could help to develop and support literacy and communication skills, which will prepare students to function productively in a more sophisticated electronic environment.

Enjoy!

Activity: Comparing Cultures

- ◆ Nature of the activity: This is a sample ESL lesson plan that illustrates the use of Nicenet features.

- ◆ Time: Approximately 15 minutes for ICA2 setup.

Students are assigned to read about an American event, using authentic information sources available on the Internet and accessed through the Nicenet Link Sharing section. Using the asynchronous computer-mediated communication function on Nicenet, students share and discuss with classmates their findings about the American cultural event that they explored. Based on their own cultural experience and the new information they explored and discussed, students compare and contrast their native culture and American culture and publish their writing on the Document section of Nicenet.

Go to the New Assignment section and post a description of the activity:

- ◆ Good morning! Today we will explore typical American cultural events. I would like you to do the following:

  - • Go to the conferencing section and post your opinion on "What is culture?"

  - • Go to the Personal Messages section and find your group members.

  - • Group work: Go to the Link Sharing section and find the **Things to Do** link. Click on it and explore the Web site. (Students can work individually on their own computers using personal messaging for group discussion, or each group of students can work around one computer to complete the activities.)

  - • Find the information to answer the group questions that are posted in the Conferencing section.

- As a group, write a paragraph answering the questions.

- Post the paragraph under the Conferencing section.

- If you are in Group 1, read Group 4's posting. If you are in Group 4, read Group 1's posting. If you are in Group 2, read Group 3's posting. If you are in Group 3, read Group 2's posting.

- After you have read the posting, discuss it with your fellow group members and post a constructive reply.

♦ Follow-Up/Extended Activity

- Read your classmates' posting on "What is culture?" and other replies in the Conferencing section. Write a compare-and-contrast essay entitled "Comparing Cultures."

- Use the **Turn in Online** function to submit your assignment. (Teachers can access the submitted assignments in the Documents section.)

After you set up the assignment, go to Conferencing section and post the question "What is culture?" After that, post four new questions for the group work. Suggested questions might be

♦ Group 1: From the home page of http://www.tbo.com, search for "Gasparilla Festival." What is Gasparilla? What things might you see during Gasparilla? (*Note:* The search box is in the upper right-hand corner of the page.)

♦ Group 2: From the home page of http://www.tbo.com, search for "Strawberry Festival." What are the dates of the Strawberry Festival? What things might you do at the Strawberry Festival? (*Note:* The search box is in the upper right-hand corner of the page.)

♦ Group 3: From the **Things To Do** section on http://www.tbo.com, go to **Travel**. Choose an event in Tampa that will happen within the next seven days. Why would you like to go to this event? (*Note:* Use the drop-down menus on the page.)

♦ Group 4: From the **Things To Do** section of http://www.tbo.com, go to **Travel**. Choose a museum in the Tampa Bay area. Why would you like to go to this museum? (*Note:* Use the drop-down menus on the page.)

♦ Go to the **Link Sharing** section and post the link for **Things to Do** (http://www.tbo.com).

13

WebQuests

Aline Harrison

The frustration I feel at times when I use the Internet is offset by the joy I get when I successfully complete something online—when I use technology with success in my classroom.

Fourth-grade Spanish teacher

About WebQuests

In her 2005 article "Making Sense of Teaching With the Web" (available at http://legacy.cloquet.k12.mn.us), Jennifer Larva describes WebQuests as a teaching approach that provides the teacher with a framework for creating inquiry-oriented activities in which some or all of the information that learners interact with comes from resources on the Internet. There are two types of WebQuests: short term and long term. The short-term WebQuest can be completed in one to three class periods. The goal is to present and explore new topics and establish new skills. However, when the teacher aims to refine and extend knowledge and skills, a long-term WebQuest might be the way to go. It may take between one week and one month.

WebQuest Principles

♦ WebQuests are designed to be conducted as a group activity—thus, they are interactive.

♦ WebQuests support foreign language interaction; they facilitate the construction of knowledge through the provision of opportunities for collaboration, information searching, and exchanges using the target language.

♦ Using WebQuests, foreign language teachers can design developmentally appropriate activities and provide learning opportunities that are suitable for the diverse needs of language learners.

♦ WebQuests are a great opportunity to use meaningfully new technology to plan, teach, and manage the learning process.

♦ WebQuests lead to critical thinking and the development of research skills.

Just try this!

Step 1   Getting started: Building blocks of a WebQuest

- Introduction—Orients and raises interest in the learners about what is coming

- Task—Describes the final outcomes of the exercise

- Process—Indicates to the learners the steps they need to follow to accomplish the task

- Evaluation—Evaluates the task

- Conclusion—Brings closure to the exercise and extends learning to other domains by encouraging reflection

If you are a novice at using technology, Microsoft Word and Microsoft PowerPoint are the easiest programs to operate in creating your own WebQuest. More advanced users may opt to use HyperStudio or HTML. You may also use one of the templates found on the Web site of San Diego State University Educational Technology Department: http://webquest.sdsu.edu/LessonTemplate.html.

Step 2   Creating a WebQuest introduction

The following is an example of how your introduction page might look.

Note: In this chapter, Cheryl J. Cox's Cinco de Mayo, A Grade 2–3 WebQuest will be used as an example. This WebQuest is available at http://www.zianet.com/cjcox/edutech4learning/cinco.html.

- Open a new document in Word or PowerPoint to begin creating a WebQuest, or sign on to a free Web page template creator.

- Create an introductory page following the model just given. Suggested elements include the following:

  - Title of the WebQuest

  - Link to the Student section

  - Link to the Teacher's Notes section

- Link to the Rubrics section

♦ Go to a second page to complete the introduction.

The introduction is a short paragraph that presents the WebQuest activity or the lesson to the students. You can create a scenario that guides students through the activity and makes it more engaging (e.g., "You are a marine scientist who is searching for the Enchanted Dolphins."). In the introduction, you should communicate the guiding question of the activity (e.g. "Who are the Enchanted Dolphins? How are they different from the sea dolphins?"). This guiding question is the focus of the whole WebQuest.

Step 3　Creating the WebQuest task

Open another page in the application you are using (PowerPoint, Word, or Web) to write the task. The task may take more than one page. Be clear in your description of the task.

Write a clear and concise description of the activity's end result. Susan Brooks and Bill Byles, the authors of the WebQuest Page (available at http://www.internet4classrooms.com/lesson-template.htm#Introduction), provide the following ideas for WebQuest tasks:

♦ A problem or mystery to be solved

♦ A position to be formulated and defended

♦ A product to be designed

♦ A complexity to be analyzed

♦ A personal insight to be articulated

♦ A summary to be created

♦ A creative work for a specific subject area

Describe all of the tools and resources that the students will need to create their project (i.e., Internet, Microsoft Word, Excel, PowerPoint, etc.). This is not the place to present the steps to be followed in the activity—you will do that in the Process section.

Now Try This

♦ Create a brief description for the organization of your WebQuest. Consider the number of class periods that you plan to spend on this lesson. Indicate whether this is a short- or long-term WebQuest. For interdisciplinary and multidisciplinary tasks, indicate which disciplines are involved.

♦ Describe how students are expected to complete the WebQuest (individually, in groups, in class, or at home).

♦ Try to predict and describe any difficulties or misconceptions that might hinder students' completion of the task and advise students on how to avoid them.

Note: The Teacher Script Page provides you with space to store and access a printable script for facilitating the process of WebQuest task completion. This might be a good approach to doing WebQuests if your learners are pre-readers or if only one computer is available in the classroom.

Step 4   Create the WebQuest resources

One of the most important sections in a WebQuest is the Resources page. This is where you will place the preselected Web sites that you want students to visit to accomplish the WebQuest task. By preselecting Web sites, you guarantee that students will research Web sites that you have already previewed and rated for their pedagogical suitability and appropriateness.

Step 5   Creating the WebQuest process

This section describes the steps that the students need to complete in order to answer the guiding question posed in the introduction. To make your description easier to read and follow, number the steps of the procedure. The Process section allows you to create a guide for the process that students will follow. Describe the steps using the second person—after all, your main audience is the students who will be completing the task. The following is an example:

1. You will be working in a team of three people.

2. Pick a role in the team (provide a description of each role)....

Continue with your explanation of the process, providing as many steps as the process requires. As students go through the process,

- Learners will access and investigate the Web sites that you have linked to your WebQuest.

- You may decide to have different groups access different Web sites on the Internet.

- Make sure to provide instructions on how students should organize the information they gather. For example, they may be required to use flowcharts, summary tables, concept maps, compare-and-contrast diagrams, etc.

- Use scaffolding strategies: To support the learning process, you may incorporate interactive activities and quizzes using Hot Potatoes (http://hotpot.uvic.ca/) or QuizStar (http://quizstar.4teachers.org/). You may also use visual organizers. The following link offers a good example: http://projects.edtech.sandi.net/staffdev/tpss98/VisualOrganizers1.gif.

Step 6   Creating the WebQuest evaluation

The evaluation is an important element of each lesson—it will tell you whether the WebQuest was successful. In this section, you will tell your students how they will be evaluated: State the products or performances that you expect them to complete or create and what your evaluation criteria are.

One of the best ways to assess students is by creating a rubric or checklist. You can find a sample of a rubric that provides assessment criteria for WebQuest activities at http://teachers.teach-nology.com/cgi-bin/webquest.cgi.

Step 7 Creating the WebQuest conclusion

This section summarizes in a few sentences what the students will have accomplished or learned. Rhetorical questions or links to sites can push students to think further about the topic and guide them if they decide to continue studying the content area beyond your WebQuest.

Now you are getting it!

Step 1 Create a WebQuest

♦ Create a WebQuest for your foreign language class using building blocks such as an introduction (a short description of your WebQuest topic), task (the activity to be completed), resources (the resources necessary to complete the task), process (the activities), evaluation (a simple rubric for evaluation), and conclusion (a paragraph about the WebQuest topic and activities).

♦ A short-cut: Templates provide an easy way to get started creating your WebQuest. If you do not want to use a template, use Microsoft Word or PowerPoint. To see other WebQuests and to create a WebQuest using a template, go to http://instantprojects.org/webquest/main.php.

You have got something to smile about!

Step 2 Write an introduction

♦ Open a page in Word or PowerPoint and start writing the introduction. If you are using a template, write the introduction in the template. You can present the topic and the project in a short paragraph that introduces the activity to the students.

♦ Be creative—remember, you want to motivate your students!

Step 3 Create tasks for students

◆ Provide specific questions to guide students through the process of completing the task.

◆ Describe the task in detail and assign roles to students if it is a group activity.

Step 4 Outline the process

◆ Describe the specific steps that your students need to take to accomplish the task.

◆ Give students direction on their roles. Be sure that the roles are clear and the directions are specific.

◆ Offer scaffolding strategies.

◆ Offer suggestions on how to present the information.

Step 5 Identify resources

◆ Offer students other sources of information that might be helpful in the process of completing the task.

◆ Check to see that links are working.

Step 6 Evaluation

◆ Provide students with a clear understanding of how they will be evaluated.

◆ Provide a rubric with the grading criteria.

Step 7 Conclusion

◆ Probe students with higher-order questions.

◆ Ask students, "What is next?"

Tricks and Traps

◆ **Trap:** Broken URLs.

  • **Trick:** Web links are sometimes broken or have been taken off the Internet. Check links prior to class and have a backup plan. The backup plan can include links to be used in case the assigned ones do not work. Have these printed on a paper just in case they are needed.

- **Trap:** Limited number of computers.
  - **Trick:** Plan WebQuests for the number of computers available if the assignment will be completed during class time. You may divide students into groups or guide the WebQuest activity yourself if there is only one computer available.

- **Trap:** Spending too much time searching Web sites.
  - **Trick:** After you have selected your topic, use search engines to structure your search. Bookmark good Web sites for future WebQuests.

Reflections

- What skills do I need to create a WebQuest lesson?

- Why should I create a WebQuest when so many are available on the Web?

- What goals can I achieve by assigning students to create a WebQuest?

- What technical training do my students need to feel comfortable doing WebQuests?

- What are the things I should consider and prepare for a WebQuest lesson?

Be sure to include the following components in a WebQuest:

- Introduction

- Task

- Process

- Evaluation

- Conclusion

Activity 1: Design a Menu for Your Foreign Language Class

- Nature of the activity: Collaborative work focused on culture. This activity can be a culminating activity or an introductory activity in a section on food. Students create a menu from a particular country. This provides a creative way for students to learn the names of foods and drinks from a particular culture. The end product will be a menu that will be presented orally, giving practice in the target language.

In a content-based foreign language classroom, students can investigate which foods are imported or exported.

- Type of activity: This pair activity allows students to focus on one cultural aspect of a particular country—food.

- Proficiency level: Advanced beginning to advanced fluency.

- Time: Approximately 1hour.

- Skills: Speaking, reading, and writing skills in the target language, with a focus on culture.

The teacher divides the students into pairs and assigns each pair to a computer with Internet access. The instructions are passed out and explained. Students work on the WebQuest. The teacher can offer ideas as students collaborate. Students print a menu, present it orally to the class, and display it in class.

Note: Depending on the class specifics—size, level of proficiency, etc.—the teacher may conduct this activity in groups of three or four students.

Standards met in this activity...	
ACTFL Standards	ISTE NETS Standards
2.1, 3.1, 4.2	II-C, III-A

Activity 2: Recipes From Around the World

- Nature of the activity: Collaborative work focused on culture. In a content-based foreign language class, students can use Web resources to compile recipes from around the world. They explain why they chose particular recipes, presenting the information both orally and in writing. Presentations facilitate the use of technology, for example, through PowerPoint.

- Type of activity: This pair activity allows students to focus on one cultural aspect of a particular country—food.

- Proficiency level: Advanced beginning to advanced fluency.

- Time: About 1hour.

- Skills: Speaking, reading, and writing skills in the target language, with a focus on culture.

The teacher divides the students into pairs and assigns each pair to a computer with Internet access. The instructions are passed out and explained. Students work on the WebQuest. The teacher can offer ideas as students collaborate. Students print their recipes, present them to the class, and display them.

♦ Variation: Students compile all of the recipes to create a cookbook.

Standards met in this activity...	
ACTFL Standards	ISTE NETS Standards
1.1, 2.1, 3.1	II-C, III-A

Activity 3: Literature of a Specific Country

♦ Nature of the activity: In a content-based foreign language class, students find the literature of a specific country that relates to the foreign language they are studying (e.g., Japanese literature). They present examples in both written and oral forms.

♦ Type of activity: This pair activity allows students to focus on reading and hone their research skills.

♦ Proficiency level: Intermediate to advanced fluency.

♦ Time: Approximately 1hour.

♦ Skills: Speaking, reading, and writing skills in the target language, with a focus on reading.

The teacher divides the students into pairs and assigns each pair to a computer with Internet access. The instructions are passed out and explained. Students work on the WebQuest. The teacher can offer ideas as students collaborate. Students print examples of the literature found and present their examples to the class.

Standards met in this activity...	
ACTFL Standards	ISTE NETS Standards
1.1, 1.2, 3.2, 4.2	IV-C, III-A, VI-A

Activity 4: Radio Talk Show

♦ Nature of the activity: Create a WebQuest in which students research the current events of a country where the foreign language they are studying is used. Each group presents the information in a radio talk show format to the entire class. The class participates by asking questions.

♦ Type of activity: This group activity allows students to use all of their language skills.

♦ Proficiency level: Intermediate to advanced fluency.

- Time: Approximately 1hour.

- Skills: Speaking, reading, and writing skills in the target language, with a focus on reading and speaking.

The teacher divides the students into groups and assigns each group to a computer with Internet access. The instructions are passed out and explained. Students work on the Web-Quest. The teacher can offer ideas as students collaborate. The students present the information to the class in a radio talk show format.

- Variation: The teacher may require specific information from the students—for example, crime rates or the URLs of some international radio stations.

Standards met in this activity...	
ACTFL Standards	ISTE NETS Standards
1.1, 1.2, 1.3, 3.2, 5.2	I-C, II-C, II-D, IV-A

Activity 5: Plan a Trip to a Specific Country

- Nature of the activity: Students in a group plan a trip to a specific country. They need to consider finances, type of clothing, medications they might need, foods they might encounter, sites to visit, and cultural norms. This WebQuest ends with a presentation in both oral and written forms.

- Type of activity: This pair activity allows students to use higher-order thinking skills, along with all of their language skills.

- Proficiency level: Intermediate to advanced fluency.

- Time: Approximately 3hours.

- Skills: Speaking, reading, and writing skills in the target language, with a focus on culture.

The teacher divides the students into pairs and assigns each pair to a computer with Internet access. The instructions are passed out and explained. Students work on the WebQuest. The teacher can offer ideas as students collaborate. Students print out their trip plans, present their plans to the class, and display them in class.

- Variation: This activity can be used to create a virtual trip as well.

Standards met in this activity...	
ACTFL Standards	ISTE NETS Standards
1.1, 1.2, 1.3, 3.1, 5.2	III-B, III-C, III-D, IV-C

14

Exercise Builder: Using Hot Potatoes

Zaohui Chen

I have always had difficulty finding programs that allow me to use Chinese characters, but thankfully as time passes, I find more and more software which is Chinese-friendly.

Tenth-grade Chinese teacher

Using Electronic Exercise Builders

Hot Potatoes is exercise-building software that can be used to create interactive Web-based quizzes quickly and easily. The software is not freeware, but it is free of charge to publicly funded nonprofit educational institutions and individuals who work for these institutions. Other users may check out the licensing terms and pricing at http://www.halfbakedsoftware.com/hot_pot_licence_terms.php.

Hot Potatoes can be downloaded from http://web.uvic.ca/hrd/hotpot/. If you plan to install Hot Potatoes immediately, it is best to use the self-extractor link. Once you have completed the installation process, you can access the application from the **Start** menu.

With Hot Potatoes, you can create five types of interactive exercises.

♦ JQuiz creates a variety of question types, such as multiple-choice and short-answer.

♦ JCloze creates fill-in-the-blank exercises.

♦ JCross creates crossword puzzles that can be completed online.

♦ JMix creates jumbled-sentence exercises.

♦ JMatch creates matching or ordering exercises.

This application offers foreign language teachers the opportunity to use technology to design a variety of assessments, collect and interpret assessment data, and apply different assessment techniques in the content areas. It also offers students an opportunity to reinforce and further their knowledge of a content area through the foreign language.

Just try this!

Step 1

♦ After downloading and installing Hot Potatoes on your computer, open the program. Go to **Start > Programs > Hot Potatoes** or Click the **Hot Potatoes** icon on the desktop.

Step 2

♦ Imagine that you are going to teach a literature class on *Alice Through the Looking Glass*. You have just finished teaching Chapter 1, "Looking-Glass House," and you decide to use JQuiz to write comprehension questions. Click on the **JQuiz** icon, and the JQuiz window will appear.

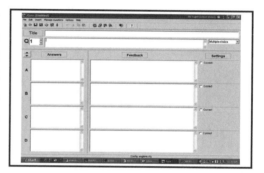

Step 3

♦ In the **Title** text field, type the title of the quiz: Comprehension Quiz on "Looking-Glass House."

♦ Type Question 1: "What is the first fault that Alice accuses the Black Kitten of?"

♦ Set the question type to **multiple choice**. To do this, use the drop-down menu on the left-hand side of the **Question Text** field.

♦ Type the answers and check off the correct answer.

- Black Kitten pulled Snowdrop away by the tail just as Alice put down the saucer of milk before her.

- Black Kitten squeaked twice while Dinah was washing its face this morning. The book is boring with no pictures or conversations. (Correct answer)

- Black Kitten unwound every bit of the worsted while Alice wasn't looking.

- Black Kitten was interrupting when Alice was talking to it.

Step 4

♦ Click the down arrow beside "Q 1" to compose Question 2.

♦ Type Question 2: "What is the way that Dinah washed her children's face?"

♦ Set the question type to **short answer**.

♦ Type the correct answer.

Step 5

♦ Click the down arrow beside "Q 2" to compose Question 3.

♦ Type Question 3: "What are the three faults that Alice accuses the Black Kitten of?"

♦ Set the question type to **multi-select**.

♦ Type the answers and check off the correct answers.

  • Black Kitten pulled Snowdrop away by the tail just as Alice put down the saucer of milk before her. (Correct)

  • Black Kitten squeaked twice while Dinah was washing its face this morning. The book is boring with no pictures or conversations. (Correct)

  • Black Kitten unwound every bit of the worsted while Alice wasn't looking. (Correct)

  • Black Kitten was interrupting when Alice was talking to it.

Step 6

♦ Follow these steps to compose more questions. (Note: You will be asked to register with Half-Baked Software in order to compose more than three questions. For detailed information, see "Tricks and Traps.")

Step 7

♦ When you finish composing all of the questions, go to the **Options** menu and select **Configure Output**. A pop-up window will appear; from this window you can

  • Put in your own subtitle and instructions

- Choose prompts and feedback to be given to students when they answer the questions (or you can put in your own prompts and feedback)

- Set a time limit for taking the quiz.

♦ By selecting the **Other** option, you can set up the way in which you would like your questions to appear on the screen—one at a time, shuffled, case sensitive, etc.

♦ If you have paid a commercial license for Hot Potatoes, you can use the CGI function to send the quiz results to your preferred e-mail account.

Step 8

♦ When you are done with all of your questions and configuration, go to **File > Save As** and save the quiz as a JQuiz file (.jqz) on your hard drive.

♦ An alternative is to save the quiz as a Web page: **File > Create Web page**. Then you can save the quiz as an HTML file.

♦ Now you can choose from several options:

- View the quiz in your browser

- Upload the file to the Hot Potatoes Web site

- Nothing

♦ The quiz viewed through your browser will look like this:

♦ If you upload the file to the Hot Potatoes Web site, you will be offered a number of steps to follow to post the quiz on the site. After you finish the steps, you will be provided with a URL that you can give your students so that they can complete the quiz.

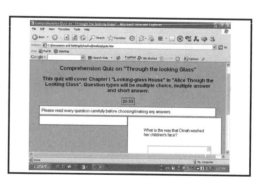

Step 9

♦ If you saved the quiz as an HTML file, you can upload the quiz to a Web site (such as Nicenet, WebCT, or Blackboard) if you have one or to a school server to make the quiz public to your students.

Step 10

♦ From the **File** menu, you can also export the quiz for printing. (The quiz will be copied to a clipboard; you can paste the quiz into a word processor and print out for classroom use.)

Now you are getting it!

Follow these steps to create your own fill-in-the-blank quiz using JCloze:

Step 11

♦ Go to **Start > Programs > Hot Potatoes** or Click the **Hot Potatoes** icon on the desktop.

♦ Click on the **JCloze** icon, and the JCloze window will open.

Step 12

♦ Type the title and the text of your quiz.

Step 13

♦ There are two ways to create blanks in the text.
1. Choose the word for which you want to create a blank that your students will fill in; double click the word to highlight. Click the **Gap** button. In the pop-up window, you can put in clue and alternate correct answers (or leave it blank to make the test more challenging). Repeat these steps until you are done with all the gaps in the text.

2. Click the **Auto Gap** button and put in a number for *n*, which meaning that every nth word will be a gap to be filled in. The text will be automatically gapped.

Step 14

♦ Gapped words will appear in red and underlined in the text.

Step 15

♦ If you want to delete gaps, click on **Clear Gaps** to delete all of the gaps in the text, or delete a particular gap by clicking **Delete Gap**.

Step 16

♦ Click **Show Words** to select a particular word and make changes such as adding clues or offering alternate correct answers.

Step 17

♦ To make the quiz easier by providing a short text summarizing the meaning of the text, go to **File > Add Reading Text**.

Step 18

To insert a picture, click on **Insert > Insert Picture from Local File**.

Step 19

♦ You can also insert a URL to allow your students to read online text when doing the quiz.

Step 20

♦ Next, configure the output for other features, such as titles, instructions, prompts and feedback, and buttons. Try it!

• Click on the **Buttons** tab and change the appearance, symbol, and captions for those buttons.

• Click on the **Appearance** tab and make changes to the colors.

Step 21

♦ When you are finished writing your exercises, you already know how to save the quiz, print it, or upload it to your Web site.

You have got something to smile about!

Step 22

♦ Open Hot Potatoes and try the other exercises.

Step 23

♦ Open JQuiz.

Step 24

♦ Go to **Options > Mode > Advanced Mode**. In Advanced Mode, you can weight each question in the quiz or set the percentage of correct answers that will be accepted.

Step 25

♦ Edit the font of the text or words by choosing **Font** from the **Options** drop-down menu.

Step 26

♦ You can also try the following:

- Add a link to the quiz

- Add a reading text to the quiz

- Edit the attributes of the reading text

Tricks and Traps

♦ **Trap:** Two Version 6 download links are offered for Windows 98/ME/NT4/2000/XP—which one should I choose?

- **Trick:** Always choose the self-extracting, auto-installing zip file instead of the plain zip file. A plain zip file requires WinZip to open, and WinZip is not freeware.

♦ **Trap:** After downloading, when I try to open and run the software, a pop-up window gives a warning such as, "The publisher could not be verified. Are you sure you want to run this software?"

- **Trick:** Go ahead and click **Run** to install the program.

♦ **Trap:** To use the Windows version of the programs, what do I need?

- **Trick:** You will need Windows 98, ME, NT4, 2000, or XP. (Windows 95 is not supported.) To use Unicode text, Windows 2000 or XP is required. A modern Web browser is also required (Internet Explorer 6+, Netscape 7+, Mozilla 1.4+, Firebird 0.7, etc.). Access to a Web server (if you wish to deliver your exercises on the Internet) or an Internet connection is needed to upload your exercises to the Hot Potatoes server.

If you know HTML and JavaScript, you can exercise more control over the final format and style of your exercise pages, but this is not a requirement for creating useful interactive pages with Hot Potatoes.

To use the exercises, your students will also need an appropriate browser. They do not need to download Hot Potatoes, however. Students using Macs can also access the exercises using Netscape, Mozilla, Safari, or Firebird.

♦ **Trap:** When I try to compose more than three questions, I am asked to register. What should I do?

• **Trick:** To register the program, fill out the form on the Web site: http://web.uvic.ca/hrd/hotpot/register.htm. Complete the form fully before submitting it. Half-baked Software will send you a key that can be used to unlock all of the features of the programs. When you receive the key, simply start one of the Potatoes (any one will do), then click on the **Help** menu and choose **Register**. Enter your username and key.

Make sure you enter the username and key exactly. The easiest way to do this is to copy and paste from the e-mail message to the registration box. Make sure you copy only the username and key—don't include the "Username:" or "Key:" bits.

Reflections

♦ What technical considerations should I take into account if I want to incorporate quizzes created in Hot Potatoes into Nicenet, WebCT, or Blackboard?

♦ What technical training do my students need to feel comfortable using Hot Potatoes–initiated quizzes?

Enjoy!

Activity 1: Mixed-Up Sentences

In teaching foreign languages, JMix can be used to design a mixed-up sentence that requires students to arrange fragments and words into correctly ordered sentences. For example, when teaching the English relative clause, the sentence "The person who sits next to me is my high-school English teacher" could be jumbled in JMix. When students complete the exercise, they will be asked to arrange the words into a grammatically correct sentence. By the way, teachers can provide alternative sentences to make the exercise less challenging in case students fail to use all of the words to make a sentence. To make the exercise more interesting, a parallel exercise can be added in the students' native language using the same language pattern (relative clause) so that students can make comparisons between the foreign language and their native language.

Standards met in this activity...	
ACTFL Standards	ISTE NETS Standards
4.1	II-A, II-B, II-E

Activity 2: City Matching

In content-based foreign language classrooms, JMatch is a good exercise builder for content knowledge reinforcement. For example, in teaching geography using a foreign language (e.g., Chinese), the matching exercise can be designed to ask students to match numbered cities on a globe with the names of cities. In this exercise, a map with numbered cities can be inserted when designing the exercise.

Standards met in this activity...	
ACTFL Standards	ISTE NETS Standards
2.1, 3.1	II-D, II-E, III-A

Activity 3: Matching Two Languages

In translation practice, JMatch can be used to design an exercise that asks students to match sentences written in the foreign language and in the native language.

Standards met in this activity...	
ACTFL Standards	ISTE NETS Standards
4.1, 4.2	II-A, III-A

Activity 4: Grammar

Practice the irregular verbs *estar* and *ser* and the subjunctive mood using J-Mix.

Standards met in this activity...	
ACTFL Standards	ISTE NETS Standards
4.1	II-A, III-A

Activity 5: Crossword

In content-based French classes—say, a math class—after teaching vocabulary, use JCross to design a crossword exercise to review the vocabulary for measurements in French.

Standards met in this activity...	
ACTFL Standards	**ISTE NETS Standards**
2.1, 3.1	II-D, II-E, III-A

Section V

E-Assessment

15

Electronic Portfolios

Rui Cheng

I always remind myself…technology is like climbing a hill.…At the beginning it all looks very daunting, but when you are at the top…you are REALLY at the top and the technology one has infused into the classroom makes life so much easier, I often wonder why I didn't get into it before now.

Eighth-grade German teacher

About E-Portfolios in the Foreign Language Classroom

Portfolios can be used by school teachers as an alternative method of assessment. This kind of assessment provides students with the opportunity to showcase their school-made products in a more relaxed manner, reducing the anxiety of many students. In today's computerized world, it is easy to create a portfolio in an electronic format. E-portfolios have gained tremendous recognition and popularity among learners and instructors, including those in the field of foreign languages. Electronic portfolios offer many advantages: They save space, allow students to develop a durable portfolio, provide easy access to materials, gives learners an opportunity to develop computer skills alongside their language skills.

In short, e-portfolios enable foreign language learners to demonstrate growth in their learning and track their progress and give students a flexible medium in which to express themselves. E-portfolios can also involve parents and teachers in students' foreign language learning.

Just try this!

Students can follow these steps to create an e-portfolio:

♦ Get the materials ready

♦ Collect the artifacts to be put into the e-portfolio.

- Show your personality in the portfolio design. Graphics, fonts, and WordArt can be used to add style to the portfolio.

- Identify the portfolio artifacts and store them in a single folder on a hard disk, server, or the Internet. You may need to scan materials that are available in hard copy only.

- Set up an electronic folder on your hard drive, floppy disk, or sever to store and organize the artifacts.

- Use multimedia to add style and individuality to your portfolio. For example, use a scanner to digitize images or use a microphone and sound digitizing program to create audio artifacts.

Now you are getting it!

- Open a Microsoft Excel spreadsheet and name it. You may use any other spreadsheet program you have available. (Check out the free Google spreadsheet available at http://www.google.com.)

- Across the top row, identify the contents of each column—for example, "Poems," "Essays," "Illustrations with Explanations," and "Audio Recordings."

- List the artifacts in the first column. For example, under "Audio Recordings," you might have audio files of recorded dialogues in which the student participated, recordings of the student reading text in the target language, singing, etc. Assign a name to each audio file.

You have got something to smile about!

- Next, hyperlink the names of the artifacts to the actual electronic version of each artifact or assignment on your computer.

- Highlight the cell in which you want to create a hyperlink.

- Select **Insert > Hyperlink**.

- A pop-up window will appear. From here, you can navigate to the file to which you want to link and click **OK**.

- If there is text in the cell in which you inserted a hyperlink, this text will be hyperlinked to the file. If there is no text in the cell, the path to the file will appear. It is a good idea to name each link.

- To follow the hyperlink, click on the cell. The document will open.

- Be sure that the files you use in the portfolio are saved in the same folder as the Excel document. This way, if you burn the portfolio folder to a CD, all of the files will be accessible.

- Hyperlink each cell to its corresponding document in the same folder.

Tricks and Traps

- **Trap:** My class has done a lot of activities. How do I select the most appropriate to include in the e-portfolio?

  - **Trick:** What you include in the e-portfolio will depend on the theme of the e-portfolio, the requirements of the program, and sometimes personal preferences. If the e-portfolio is required by the program, all of the required work needs to be included in it. If you have other work that you are proud of but is not required, you can set up your own personal e-portfolios with different topics and themes. If the e-portfolio is a class project as part of an assessment, you can include work that shows progress, acquisition of new language points, and other work that shows students' efforts in the study.

- **Trap:** There are so many types of technology available. Which one should I use to create my e-portfolios?

  - **Trick:** It is true that there are many types of technology available, and more and more are coming to market. For e-portfolios, technology is not the most important concern. You can use the technology that is available and familiar to you to create your e-portfolios. The content of the e-portfolios is more important than the technology used to create them. Remember, Excel is always at your disposal. Yet it is sometimes fun to learn new technologies and try them out in the creation of your e-portfolios.

- **Trap:** Many teachers like to use e-portfolios as one means of assessment. How can students also keep portfolios that are personal?

  - **Trick:** E-portfolios are useful for both schoolwork and personal interests, such as hobbies. One e-portfolio can be created for schoolwork that will be assessed by the teacher. Another e-portfolio can be created for personal interests. Actually, many e-portfolios can be created to represent different themes in students' studies and lives.

- **Trap:** E-portfolios seem very interesting. I am just scared of the technological complexity? What can I do?

- **Trick:** There are many advanced technologies that are out of reach for many of us. However, there are also many simple technologies that are easy to learn and easy to use. If advanced technology is out of your reach, one or more simple technologies can be used to create e-portfolios.

- ◆ **Trap:** How can my students make the home page for their portfolio more creative and expressive?

- **Trick:** PowerPoint can be used instead of Excel. PowerPoint allows for designing attractive slides with images and multiple colors. Just open a slide and organize the names of your links in a table or a list. Insert hyperlinks in the same way that you did in Excel.

Reflections

- ◆ How can I use e-portfolios to encourage participation from all students?

- ◆ How can I use e-portfolios to promote productive skills?

- ◆ How can I use e-portfolios to motivate students' foreign language learning?

- ◆ How can I use e-portfolios to assess students' performance?

- ◆ How can I use e-portfolios to activate students' best performance?

Enjoy!

Activity 1: Creating an E-Portfolio of Students' Personal Lives

- ◆ Nature of the activity: Creative individual work.

- ◆ Type of activity: This can be a whole-class activity completed in the computer lab or an individual activity completed at home. The goal is for students to use the target language creatively to set up an e-portfolio of their personal interests.

- ◆ Proficiency level: Advanced beginning to advanced fluency.

- ◆ Time: This activity can be done in class or as a homework assignment. If it is done in class, it will take approximately one hour. Students can continue building their portfolio in their spare time. If it is done as a homework assignment, it can last much longer depending on what students choose to include and the technology they use.

- ◆ Skills: Writing in the target language.

♦ Additional materials: Dictionary.

The teacher introduces several simple technologies, such as Microsoft Word and Excel. The teacher demonstrates how to set up an e-portfolio in the target language and asks students to create their own e-portfolios to showcase their personal interests using the target language. Technical and language problems can be addressed by the teacher upon request.

Standards met in this activity...	
ACTFL Standards	**ISTE NETS Standards**
1.2, 1.3, 5.1, 5.2	II-C, D, III-C

Activity 2: Creating an E-Portfolio on the History of Students' Foreign Language Study

♦ Nature of the activity: Collaborative or individual.

♦ Type of activity: This can be a whole-class activity or an individual activity.

♦ Proficiency level: Advanced beginning to advanced fluency.

♦ Time: This activity can be done in class or as a homework assignment. The time is unlimited, as you can ask students to continue adding new information in this e-portfolio.

♦ Skills: Reading and writing in the target language.

The teacher asks students to reflect on their foreign language studies and to find work they have done at each level of study. Students select representative works at each stage to include in their e-portfolios. The teacher can encourage the students to write a short reflection on each work describing what they learned.

Standards met in this activity...	
ACTFL Standards	**ISTE NETS Standards**
1.2, 1.3, 5.1, 5.2	II-C, II-D, V-C

Activity 3: Creating an E-Portfolio to Showcase Students' Presentations and Papers

♦ Nature of the activity: Individual or collaborative work.

♦ Type of activity: This can be a whole-class or individual activity.

♦ Proficiency level: Advanced beginning to advanced fluency.

- Time: This activity can be done in class or as a homework assignment. If it is done in class, it will take approximately one hour. If it is done as a homework assignment, it can last much longer depending on what students choose to include and the technology they use.

- Skills: Reading in the target language.

The teacher asks the students to organize and sort their presentations and papers done in the target language. Students choose representative works from their presentations and papers. If the presentations and papers are not in an electronic format, students will need to convert them into an electronic format first. Students create their e-portfolios in the target language, including the electronic versions of their selected papers and presentations.

Standards met in this activity...	
ACTFL Standards	ISTE NETS Standards
1.2, 1.3, 5.1, 5.2, 2.1, 2.2	II-D, III-B, III-C

Activity 4: Sharing E-Portfolios With Other Students

- Nature of the activity: Creative collaborative work.

- Type of activity: This is a whole-class activity.

- Proficiency level: Advanced beginning to advanced fluency.

- Time: This activity can be done in class or as a homework assignment. If it is done in class, it will take approximately 30 minutes. If it is done as a homework assignment, it can last much longer depending on students' interest in sharing their works with peers.

- Skills: Reading and writing in the target language.

The teacher asks the students to complete e-portfolios in the target language on a specific topic. The teacher can ask the students to allow other students in the class to access their portfolios. Students read each other's e-portfolios and provide feedback to their peers.

Standards met in this activity...	
ACTFL Standards	ISTE NETS Standards
1.2, 1.3, 5.1, 5.2	II-D, III-B, III-C

16

Electronic Surveys: Inquiring With Authentic Language

Ruth Ban and Jane Harvey

I never liked assessment, evaluation or tests...whatever you call it for a teacher who makes it up or a student who takes it, they are always burdensome. Technology helps ease the pain of it all, from all perspectives.

12th-grade Latin teacher

Electronic Surveys in the Foreign Language Classroom

The use of electronic surveys in the foreign language learning process provides a real-world opportunity for students to use their new language skills. This tool has applications in the business world and among interest groups, teachers, and other professionals who create surveys to gain information about a group of people. These uses can easily be transferred to the language classroom, where both students and teachers look for answers to questions about content and language. For example, one aspect of language learning is to gain cultural knowledge about speakers of the target language. This type of tool can be used to gain insight into cultural practices by exchanging surveys with teachers in other parts of the world.

Because this tool is readily available, user friendly, and free to users, it can easily be adapted for classroom use. Within the classroom, it offers teachers an opportunity to inquire into students' opinions about content as well as the learning process.

Just try this!

Survey tools such as SurveyMonkey allow students to apply the foreign language knowledge they have gained in the classroom to find out about the content matter, their classmates, teachers, schoolmates, or other groups of people. This tool can be used to inquire into the likes and dislikes, preferences, frequency of activities, and opinions of a particular group of people.

This chapter shows you how to create a basic survey for your students and provides guidelines for teaching students how to create their own surveys. Note that SurveyMonkey has both free and paid versions.

Step 1 Finding the Web site

♦ Type http://www.surveymonkey.com into your browser and click on **Signup Now** at the bottom of the page. This will take you to a page where you can create a new account.

Step 2 Creating an account

♦ On this page, create an account by filling in your e-mail address and choosing a password. Optional information is requested that you can provide if you choose.

Step 3 Starting a new survey

♦ At the top of the next screen, click on **New Survey**. Then choose **From Scratch** and click on **Next**.

Step 4 Designing your survey

♦ Click on the **Theme** drop-down menu to choose the color scheme that you want to use.

Step 5 Developing your survey

♦ Click on **Edit Title**. On the next screen, type in the title of your survey. You can choose to have your title visible or hidden from people taking the survey. You can also name the navigation links in your survey. For example, you could label the links in the language you are teaching. When finished, click on **Update** (the link is in the upper right-hand corner).

Step 6 Naming your page

♦ To give your page a name, click on **Edit Page** and add a title. There is also space to include a short description of the page. Now you are ready to start entering your survey questions.

Step 7 Creating survey questions

♦ Click on **Add Question** and select the type of question you want to ask from the drop-down menu. Let's choose **Choice—One Answer (Vertical)** to begin with. On the next screen, type in your question and several possible answers. On this page, you have a choice to add a text field in which the respondent can enter his or her own answer. Then click **Add**. (Note: The features that allow you to randomize multiple-choice answers or allow respondents to leave questions unanswered are not available in the free version of SurveyMonkey.)

♦ Next, add as many questions as you like.

Step 8 Creating horizontal questions

♦ If you choose **Choice—One Answer (Horizontal)**, the answer options will be displayed horizontally. (Note: You can see what your survey questions will look like by clicking on **Preview** at the bottom right-hand corner of the screen.)

Step 9 Administering the survey

♦ Now you are ready to administer the survey! On the Surveys page, click on the **Collect** icon of the survey you want to administer.

♦ From this page, you can create a link to send to survey participants by e-mail. Click on the **Create** to create an e-mail message icon.

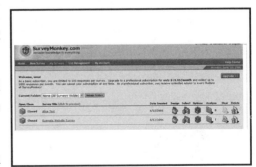

♦ You will see a box with a Web site address on it. You can cut and paste this into the e-mail message that you will send to your students to invite them to take your survey.

Step 10 — Setting survey options

♦ On the Surveys page, click on the **Options** icon. On this page, you can allow students to respond only once or many times or to go back to the survey once they have finished.

Step 11 — Viewing the results of the survey

♦ To view the results of the survey, click on the **Analyze** icon, and a visual representation of the results of the survey will appear.

Step 12 — Viewing details

♦ You can see individual answers by clicking on **View** detail in the top right-hand corner of the page.

♦ These have guided you and your students through the process of creating and analyzing basic surveys. Now you will learn to use more complex question types.

Now you are getting it!

Step 13 — Writing matrix questions (choices displayed in a matrix format)

♦ Begin by creating a new survey (see Steps 1–6). To add a matrix question to your survey, click on **Add Question**. On the drop-down menu, choose **Matrix— One Answer per Row (Rating Scale)**. This question style is good for "How often?" or "How much?" questions. Type in the questions and click **Add**. Remember, you can always edit your questions by clicking **Edit Question**.

Step 14 — Viewing the results of the survey

♦ To view the results of the survey, click on the **Analyze** icon.

Step 15 — Writing questions with menu options

♦ From the **Add Question** drop-down menu, choose **Matrix—Multiple Answers per Rows (Menu)**. Type the question in the text box and name the rows.

♦ Scroll down to choose the number of menu items. Give the menu a heading and write the menu choices.

- Add your new question.

This question type is useful if you want to offer the same responses to different questions.

Step 16 Viewing the results of this question

- To view the results of the survey, click on the **Analyze** icon

You have got something to smile about!

Step 17 Creating open-ended questions

- From the **Add Question** drop-down menu, choose **Open-ended—One line with Prompt**.

Step 18 Viewing the results of this question

- To view the results of the survey, click on the **Analyze** icon. Although this type of question seems to be the easiest question type to create, it is the most difficult to analyze. The results can vary from complete sentences to one-word answers.

- If students use this question type, the teacher must scaffold their use of both language and higher-order thinking skills.

Tricks and Traps

- **Trap:** It takes a long time to create a survey. Do I have to create a new one every time?

  - **Trick:** You can reuse the same survey by clearing the results. To do this, click on the **Clear** icon on the Surveys page. This clears students' responses but leaves the questions intact.

- **Trap:** Students cannot access the survey.

  - **Trick:** No one except the creator of the survey can access the survey if it is closed. To make sure the survey is open, go to the Surveys page and look at the box to the left of the survey title. If the box is closed, simply click on it to open it.

- ♦ **Trap:** I want to edit my survey, but I can't get into the editing page.

  - • **Trick:** A survey can only be edited if it is closed. On the Surveys page, make sure the box next to the survey title is closed.

- ♦ **Trap:** There are a lot of choices for matrix questions.

  - • **Trick:** You may need to experiment with this type of question because there are so many options. A good way to experiment is to type nonsense words in the options and click **Add**. This will give you a chance to see what the question will look like. You can always delete the question after previewing it.

Reflections

- ♦ What kind of technology skills will my students need to use this tool?

- ♦ How can I plan these sessions to make them motivating and interesting to the students?

- ♦ How can I design a survey for my students that will provoke higher-order thinking, as well as integrate the grammar, language functions, and vocabulary items in our present unit?

- ♦ How can I use surveys to enhance my students' foreign language skills?

Activity 1: The Weather

- ♦ In this activity, students discuss the weather in their hometowns and in other parts of the country.

- ♦ Form collaborative groups.

- ♦ Have students create questions about the weather, the seasons, and favorite activities during the different seasons in their hometowns. Invite them to inquire into people's experiences with weather in different parts of the world. Remind them to use questions such as "Have you ever…," "What would you like to do if…" to ask about living in places where the weather is extreme or different from the weather where your class lives.

- ♦ Have groups work together to create and post surveys. Invite teachers in your school, district, or county to respond to your students' surveys.

- ♦ Set aside time in your class period(s) for the groups to report orally on their findings. Invite open discussion about the results.

Standards met in this activity...	
ACTFL Standards	**ISTE NETS Standards**
1.1, 1.2, 1.3, 3.1	II-C, D, III-C

Activity 2: Learning a Foreign Language— A Teacher-Created Survey

♦ In this activity, students reflect on their language learning processes and those of other language learners.

♦ Based on current research on how language is learned, create questions that encourage students to reflect on their language learning process. For example, questions might focus on strategies such as using cognates to develop vocabulary, advance planning when faced with oral production, or social interaction to practice language.

♦ Develop questions and create a survey. Post your survey and invite your students to participate. Consider allowing anonymous postings to permit total honesty in the responses.

♦ After collecting the responses, distribute them to the class and invite discussion about ways to make foreign language learning easier.

Standards met in this activity...	
ACTFL Standards	**ISTE NETS Standards**
4.1	II-C

Activity 3: Holidays and Celebrations

♦ In this activity, students investigate holidays that are observed and celebrated by students in other cultures.

♦ Work with a teacher in your school or in another school who knows students who speak the target foreign language. Invite his or her group to respond to your students' questions about holidays. If possible, invite speakers of the target language from different countries so that cultural practices can be compared.

♦ Have students create questions about the nature of the holiday and the way it is celebrated. Tell them to create the survey using the questions they have written. Have them post the survey.

♦ After the survey has been answered, have students retrieve the analyzed data. Have them create posters that discuss their findings. Invite parents, other students, teachers, and school administrators to attend the poster exhibit.

Standards met in this activity...	
ACTFL Standards	**ISTE NETS Standards**
1.1, 1.2, 1.3, 3.1	II-C, II-D, III-C

Activity 4: School Favorites

♦ In this activity, students discover "school favorites."

♦ Divide students into collaborative groups. Have students choose a "favorite," such as a favorite color, movie, or type of music.

♦ Have each group write questions about their "favorite." When each group has finished their questions, have the groups integrate their questions and create a survey.

♦ Post the surveys. Invite other foreign language classes to respond to survey.

♦ Have each group retrieve the results from their questions. Tell them to use the results to write a paragraph on the "school favorites." Have them take a process approach to their writing by writing a rough draft, revising, editing, rereading, and finally publishing their work. Explore the possibility of publishing their work in the target language in the school or local newspaper, both in print and electronically.

Standards met in this activity...	
ACTFL Standards	**ISTE NETS Standards**
1.1, 1.2, 1.3, 5.1	II-C, II-D, III-C

Activity 5: Test Your Knowledge

♦ In this activity, students gain knowledge about the countries where the target language is spoken. It offers a forum for other students to test and acquire knowledge about these countries.

♦ Form collaborative groups and have each group choose a country in which the target language is spoken. Tell students to do library or Internet research on the assigned country. Remind them to find out about population, geography, economy, weather, customs, and so on.

- Have the groups create a survey based on the information they learned about the country. Remind them that they must provide incorrect options as well as correct options if they are testing people's knowledge.

- Have groups post their surveys. Invite other groups to test their knowledge of these countries.

- Provide an oral or written forum for students to report on the results of their surveys. If the surveys reports misinformation about a country, invite students to propose means for informing the school community.

Standards met in this activity...	
ACTFL Standards	ISTE NETS Standards
1.1, 1.2, 1.3, 2.1, 2.2, 4.2, 5.2	II-C, II-D, III-C

Activity 6: The Most Popular

- In this activity, students find out about the most popular personalities and activities in a country where the target language is spoken. It is a good opportunity to practice superlative forms. For the activity to work best, students need to have access to a school or class in the country in which the target language is spoken.

- Form collaborative groups and invite the students to research a list of popular personalities and activities from the target culture.

- Have the groups construct surveys to find out which personalities and activities are most popular among the young people of the target culture.

- Have students post their surveys and get responses from the students in the target culture school.

- Invite the groups to prepare a class presentation on what they have found.

- Invite follow-up discussion to compare the personalities and activities of the target culture to those of the students' own culture.

Standards met in this activity...	
ACTFL Standards	ISTE NETS Standards
1.1, 1.2, 1.3, 2.1, 2.2, 4.2, 5.2	II-C, II-D, III-C

Activity 7: Feedback on the Class

- One of the best ways to reflect on and improve your teaching is to get feedback from students on your lessons and the ways they are being asked to learn. This activity gives teachers an opportunity to find out about students' feelings about the class.

♦ Based on your beliefs and current practices, construct a survey asking for students' reactions to the activities and curriculum of the class. Make sure that you ask for positive contributions, such as questions beginning with "What are the things you most like about…?"

♦ Post the survey and allow students to respond anonymously.

♦ You can either report the results of the survey to students or use what you learn to make changes in your teaching practices.

♦ If students' responses show a lack of understanding of useful teaching and learning strategies, it may be worthwhile to spend some class time discussing the rationale for such strategies.

Standards met in this activity…	
ACTFL Standards	**ISTE NETS Standards**
1.1, 1.2, 1.3, 2.1, 2.2, 4.2, 5.2	II-C, II-D, III-C

Activity 8: First Steps in Asking Questions

♦ This activity is aimed at beginning students who are just learning how to form questions in the target language.

♦ Form pairs of students and ask them to write 5–10 questions that they would like to ask other students in the school. These questions could be about daily habits, likes and dislikes, and so on.

♦ Have the pairs of students create a survey based on their questions and then post their surveys.

♦ Invite students from other classes to respond to these surveys, especially students from classes of higher levels of the target language.

♦ When they get their results, the pairs should write a paragraph about what they learned from their surveys. These paragraphs could be revised, edited, and posted in the classroom or in the school corridor.

♦ Invite the students who responded to the survey to view the results.

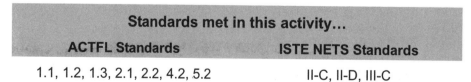

Standards met in this activity…	
ACTFL Standards	**ISTE NETS Standards**
1.1, 1.2, 1.3, 2.1, 2.2, 4.2, 5.2	II-C, II-D, III-C

Section VI

Taking Your Own Journey

17

Using Technology-Enhanced Activities to Facilitate Second-Language Learning

Tony Erben

The activities presented in this chapter combine all of the technologies and software that have been introduced in this book. Although the research indicates some broadly accepted understandings of what a technology-enhanced foreign language classroom should look like, the jury is still out on the effectiveness of technology in the language acquisition process. However, the question is not so much *whether* technology should be used but *how* and *when* it should be used. Much interesting research has focused on the areas of instructional technology and second language acquisition. From this research, what is clear is that when technology and the curriculum are connected in meaningful ways, foreign language students are more efficient, more effective, more motivated, and have greater access to the foreign language than students learning in a technology-deprived classroom. With the proper implementation of technology, foreign language students can pick up language skills faster and with less effort, retain language knowledge longer, obtain foreign language materials easier, achieve interactions with native speakers more fortuitously, learn through a wider range of modes, and engage in exploratory, experiential, and communicative tasks in a far wider range of disparate locations than just the classroom.

Foreign language learning is about communication, and half the teacher's job is to teach students how to be good communicators in the foreign language. When technology is used to facilitate interaction, this is called computer-mediated communication (CMC). What we know from research on CMC gives us great hope and opportunity in the foreign language classroom. For example, learners' self-reported anxiety is lower (Beauvois, 1992; Kelm,

1992), student participation (Chun, 1994) and peer-to-peer interaction (Kern, 1995) are greater, learners have greater cultural awareness, and there is more online discourse than in regular face-to-face classroom interaction (Cubillos, 1998). Gonglewski (1999) and Salaberry (1996) have found that students who use online communication are more aware of their errors. Warschauer (1996) indicates that students who participate in online discussions have more coherent and cohesive discourse. Overall, the benefits of CMC include positive learner attitudes and motivation (Bradley & Lomicka, 2000); increased student participation, even among students who tend to be marginalized (Bump, 2000); increased learner collaboration (Gonzalez-Edflet, 1990); and increased language production with a variety of discourse functions in synchronous mode (Chun, 1994; Sotillo, 2000) and with syntactically more complex language output in asynchronous mode (Sotillo, 2000).

Finally, the use of multimedia (text, motion video, photo images, sound, and graphics controlled by computer) complements communicative language learning through its potential to enhance students' learning experiences. While interacting with multiple forms of media, students are more motivated to engage with more complex issues than they are with simple drill-and-kill exercises. Multimedia supports contextualized learning and prepares students to apply what they have learned in an appropriate context (Reeves, 1992). As such, the computer is not the central focus of the activity but supports the teacher and learner.

Activity 1: The Ten Commandments

- ◆ Technology resources: Classroom with one or more computers or computer lab

- ◆ Technology type: Sound files

- ◆ Nature of the activity: Vocabulary building

- ◆ Task type: Following commands

- ◆ Proficiency level: Any

- ◆ Preparation and resources: Recording sound files, burning files onto a CD

- ◆ Time: 15 minutes

- ◆ Participant structure: Pairs

- ◆ Learning-how-to-learn skill: Giving and following instructions

Procedure

The teacher records a range of commands as sound files on his or her computer—for example, "touch something soft," "walk to the wall," "pick up your folders," etc. At least 40 different commands should be recorded. Once this is done, the teacher burns the individual sound files onto a CD and transfers the files to the computers that the students will be using. When the class starts, the teacher divides the class into pairs. Student A makes sure Student B opens each file and carries out the first 20 commands. When Student B gets the command wrong, he or she stops. The activity continues until the last student is left. Then the roles are reversed, and Student A listens to each sound file and acts out the last 20 commands until only one student is left. The best Student A and B then square off against each other. This activity encourages the comprehension of verbs—"pick up," "touch," "grab," "bend," "turn," "wipe," "bend"—and provides an opportunity for students to familiarize themselves with sound files.

Variations

♦ Rather than giving instructions that require students to carry out physical acts, the teacher gives instructions and commands that require students to use the Internet—for example, "find a Web site on Japanese kendo" or "send your friend an e-mail message with the address of your Web site."

♦ Rather than using the sound files to practice commands, the teacher uses the chat function of Nicenet to enhance students' reading comprehension skills.

Activity 2: Catch a Word Bingo

♦ Technology resources: Classroom with one or more computers or computer lab

♦ Technology type: E-mail and chat in Nicenet class

♦ Nature of the activity: Vocabulary building

♦ Task type: Discovery learning

♦ Proficiency level: Any

♦ Preparation and resources: Choosing and e-mailing pictures to your students

♦ Time: 15 minutes

♦ Participant structure: Individual or whole class

♦ Learning-how-to-learn skill: Using an electronic thesaurus or dictionary

Procedure

♦ As students settle down in front of their computers, the teacher tells them to go to the Internet and log in to their Yahoo! Mail accounts. Earlier, the teacher e-mailed each of them a collage of pictures. The teacher instructs the students to look at the pictures and then write down (in an e-mail message) 10 adjectives that best describe the pictures.

♦ If students cannot think of 10 adjectives, the teacher directs them to use an online dictionary or thesaurus to find 10 words. The teacher tells the students to find synonyms and antonyms so as to build on their own vocabulary capital.

♦ Once the teacher has received all of the adjectives, they are compiled into one list. While doing this, the teacher instructs the students to write 10 sentences using their pictures as a starting point. They are to e-mail these sentences to the teacher as well.

♦ The teacher starts to play bingo by reading out one adjective at a time. If a student has that adjective on his or her list, it is crossed off the list. The first student to cross of all of his or her adjectives wins.

Variations

♦ Once the bingo game is complete, each student e-mails his or her pictures and adjectives to another student. Each students constructs a story based on the new picture and using the adjectives.

♦ Students are asked to describe any aspect of themselves—for example, "Choose fives nouns that describe your personality (or your physique, your clothes, etc.). Students send these words anonymously in an e-mail to one of their classmates. The receiver must guess who it is by replying with questions.

♦ The teacher chooses a set number of words, linguistic structures, or functions and paste them into a chat session in Nicenet. The teacher divides the class into pairs or groups and tells students to find the meaning of the words, structures, phrases, or functions using an online dictionary or thesaurus. When a pair or group has the answer, they are to type the meaning next to the word in a color that represents their pair or group; the teacher places a time limit on the activity. The pair or group that finds the most meanings and posts them to the chat site wins.

Activity 3: If I Was a Millionaire

♦ Technology resources: Classroom with one or more computers or computer lab

♦ Technology type: E-mail and chat in Nicenet class

♦ Nature of the activity: Imagination and story construction

♦ Task type: Guided learning

♦ Proficiency level: Any

♦ Preparation and resources: None

♦ Time: 20 minutes

♦ Participant structure: Individual or whole class

♦ Learning-how-to-learn skill: Synthesizing and processing information

Procedure

♦ This activity may be completed over an extended period of time. When a student finishes an activity earlier than the rest, he or she can log on to the computer in the classroom and go into the Nicenet class. On the discussion board there is a prompt: "Think of 10 things you would do for your school if you won a million dollars (or whatever currency suits)."

♦ The students writes his or her answers in an e-mail message and sends it to another student in the class.

♦ The student who receives the list chooses the most bizarre thing that the sender could do and posts this on the discussion board.

♦ Once the full list is written on the discussion board, guide the students in constructing a story (as a group) based on the prompts posted to the discussion board.

♦ Write the story in the chat window and construct the story sentence by sentence. The teacher may want to ask students to use specific sentence connectors or structures so as to make the story cohesive and consistent.

Activity 4: What I Know, What I Don't Know, What I'd Like to Know

♦ Technology resources: Classroom with one or more computers or computer lab

♦ Technology type: Internet

♦ Nature of the activity: Brainstorming

♦ Task type: Fill in the blanks

♦ Proficiency level: Any

♦ Preparation and resources: None

♦ Time: 10–15 minutes

♦ Participant structure: Group or whole class

♦ Learning-how-to-learn skill: Reflecting on one's knowledge base, compiling and categorizing information

Procedure

♦ The teacher chooses a topic on which a unit is based, such as holidays, family, cooking, or school.

♦ The teacher uses Microsoft PowerPoint to draw three columns titled "Words I Know," "Words I'm Not Sure About," and "Words I Want To Know."

- The student groups at each computer are asked to copy the PowerPoint slide onto their computers.

- Each group fills in the columns with as much information as they can with the aid of the Internet.

- Once each group is finished, the teacher directs each group to present what they have come up with.

- The teacher and the class review what the group knows; answers, explains, or clarifies what they don't know; and answers what they would like to know.

Variations

- The teacher displays the same table just described, but instead of asking groups to write down words they do or do not know related to the topic given, the teacher asks students to write down words related to content matter (math, social studies, science). Follow the same steps to complete the activity.

- The teacher doesn't leave it up to the students to think about the words or content that they may or may not know about a given topic. Here, the teacher provides specific words or content information and asks the students to discuss the words in a chat room and surf the Internet to find out what the terms mean and then report back to the class.

Activity 5: Find Me

- Technology resources: Classroom with one or more computers or computer lab

- Technology type: Internet, Nicenet, e-mail, chat

- Nature of the activity: Reading for understanding

- Task type: Comparing Information

- Proficiency level: Any

- Preparation and resources: Finding articles on the Internet

- Time: 10–15 minutes

- Participant structure: Individual, group, or whole class

- Learning-how-to-learn skill: Sharing information

Procedure

- The teacher locates two pieces of written information on the Internet focusing on any one topic.

- The two documents are copied into a Microsoft Word document and sent to all students as an e-mail attachment.

- The teacher divides the students into groups. The groups compare the information in the two documents and write down the similarities and differences.

- The class is then brought together by the teacher.

- Each group pastes their collective work (written in a Word document) into a third word document and posts it on Nicenet so that the whole class can read it.

- The teacher compares the groups' answers and asks the class to explore why the groups answered as they did and to engage students in a discussion of why the information given in the two documents was similar or dissimilar.

Variations

- The teacher creates a cloze exercise on the same topic using an online activity creator such as Hot Potatoes. Students are to complete the exercise as a class. Next, the teacher instructs each group to surf the Internet as a group to find a Web site with similar information. Students copy and paste the information into a Word document and create a cloze exercise using Hot Potatoes (http://hotpot.uvic.ca/) Quia (http://www.quia.com). Once completed, students send the Web address for the exercise by e-mail to other groups, who complete the exercise.

Activity 6: Chinese Whispers

- Technology resources: Classroom with one or more computers or computer lab

- Technology type: Chat

- Nature of the activity: Relay

- Task type: Competition

- Proficiency level: Any

- Preparation and resources: None

- Time: 10–15 minutes

- Participant structure: Individual or whole class

- Learning-how-to-learn skill: Recalling information

Procedure

- Chinese Whispers can be played in a number of ways: by recalling words, adding on to a sentence, constructing activities for a lesson, and so on. For example, the teacher provides a prompt, such as, "You are lost in Mexico City…" on a chat discussion board in Nicenet.

♦ Start with the linguistic structure "I would…"

Variations

♦ The whispers are conveyed using sound files.

♦ The whispers are conveyed using e-mail.

Activity 7: Aliens

♦ Technology resources: Classroom with one or more computers or computer lab

♦ Technology type: Chat

♦ Nature of the activity: Guessing

♦ Task type: Competition

♦ Proficiency level: Any

♦ Preparation and resources: None

♦ Time: 10–15 minutes

♦ Participant structure: Individual or whole class

♦ Learning-how-to-learn skill: Deducing

Procedure

In this activity, a student or a group of students at one computer must think of an object that a teacher uses every day. The teacher explains that all of the students are extraterrestrials, and the objects chosen by other students are unfamiliar to them. The students' task is to ask yes/no questions about the object. Whoever guesses the object with the least amount of questions wins.

Activity 8: Discover a Story

♦ Technology resources: Classroom with one or more computers or computer lab

♦ Technology type: Chat

♦ Nature of the activity: Asking questions

♦ Task type: Story construction

♦ Proficiency level: Any

- Preparation and resources: None

- Time: 15–20 minutes

- Participant structure: Whole class

- Learning-how-to-learn skill: Deducing

Procedure

- The aim of this activity is for students to figure out the plot of a story by asking a series of questions. First, the teacher selects a plot from a well-known story.

- The students ask yes/no questions (through chat) to figure out the plot of the story and to learn who the characters are.

- As the students discover the story line, they summarize the plot in a Microsoft Word document.

Activity 9: A Day in the Life Of…

- Technology resources: Classroom with one or more computers or computer lab

- Technology type: Chat, Web page

- Nature of the activity: Asking questions

- Task type: Story construction

- Proficiency level: Any

- Preparation and resources: None

- Time: 15–20 minutes

- Participant structure: Whole class

- Learning-how-to-learn skill: Deducing

Procedure

- In this activity, students (in groups) choose an inanimate object that is typically used during the delivery of a subject area—for example, a Bunsen burner for science, a slide rule for math, a map for geography, or a language dictionary for foreign languages.

- The objects are drawn in a Microsoft Word document or clip art is pasted into a document and sent to the class. The teacher may put the pictures up on his or her Web site and instruct the students to go to the Web site and open the document.

- Within each group, the students choose one object each from the document on the Web page. Using a prepared sound file—an icon on the Web page—the students are told that at night, these objects come alive and talk about their class. The students and are asked to think about what these objects might say, see, and hear. The teacher tells the students to think of different creative ideas.

- To motivate the students, the teacher may want to write a few suggestions on the whiteboard or in the chat window.

- Once several ideas have been discussed, the class is divided into groups and asked to construct a "Day in the life of…" story.

Variation

- Rather than ask students to construct a story, groups of students are paired with each other. Group A chooses an object, and Group B constructs questions to ask Group A about the object in question. One pair of groups may interact through the audio function, another pair of groups may interact through chat, and a third pair of groups may interact using e-mail.

Activity 10: Back-to-Front Fortune Telling

- Technology resources: Classroom with one or more computers or computer lab

- Technology type: Web page, LCD projector

- Nature of the activity: Writing and reading

- Task type: Story construction

- Proficiency level: Intermediate

- Preparation and resources: Creating a computer deck of cards on a Web page

- Time: 15–20 minutes

- Participant structure: Individual, pair, or whole class

- Learning-how-to-learn skill: Organizing information

Procedure

- In this fortune-telling activity, the teacher cuts and pastes card faces to a blank Web page. The teacher creates a hotlink for each card that goes to another blank Web page.

- Next, the teacher prepares a list of difficult situations and then writes down ways to deal with them. The students must think of strategies to deal with the situations. For example, you are lost in a foreign city, you have run out of money, your passport is out of date and you leave for Germany next week, you put a dent in your rental car. In other words, there is an explanation or strategy for every situation.

♦ For every hotlink on the Web page, the teacher creates a blank Web page and pastes in a situation or a strategy (have enough strategies and situations for each hotlink).

♦ Once completed, the teachers displays the deck of cards through an LCD on to a whiteboard.

♦ The teacher brings the class together to participate in the next phase of the activity.

♦ Here, the teacher instructs students that they are to read their own fortunes. One by one, pairs of students click on three cards, which take them to a strategy or a situation.

♦ The student reads the strategy and then predicts or describes a situation that may have led the strategy in question. Conversely, the student describes the circumstances under which he or she may have employed the strategy in question.

Variations

♦ The teacher can ask the student or group to predict, describe, or write about the circumstances under which the strategy in question might be used through the chat window function.

♦ Rather than having students about write the strategy and then predict when it might be used, the students could list the cause—for example, communication barriers—for the "fortune" and then discuss how they would overcome such problems.

♦ As homework, the students could e-mail or chat with each other about the situation or strategy; their object is to reconstruct a dialogue that could have led to the situation or strategy.

Activity 11: Jeopardy!

♦ Technology resources: Classroom with one or more computers or computer lab

♦ Technology type: Microsoft PowerPoint, LCD projector

♦ Nature of the activity: Writing and reading

♦ Task type: Competition

♦ Proficiency level: Any

♦ Preparation and resources: Creating a Jeopardy! game in PowerPoint

♦ Time: 15–20 minutes

- Participant structure: Individual, pair, or whole class

- Learning-how-to-learn skill: Creating questions

Procedure

- See http://www.d.umn.edu/~hrallis/guides/PP/pp_jeopardy/jeopardy.html.

Activity 12: Adapting Teacher Talk

- Technology resources: Classroom with one or more computers or computer lab

- Technology type: Microsoft PowerPoint and Word, LCD projector, chat, e-mail, sound

- Nature of the activity: Conversing

- Task type: Conducting a guided conversation

- Proficiency level: Any

- Preparation and resources: One-half of a dialogue

- Time: 15 minutes

- Participant structure: Individual or whole class

- Learning-how-to-learn skill: Responding to cues, filling in the blanks

Procedure

- This is a simple exercise to help students understand the functions of contextual talk, focusing on particular situations. A script of a situation is sent to students as an e-mail attachment. The script contains only half of a dialogue between two people. The conversation revolves around a specific topic.

- In pairs, students take on the role of one of the participants in the conversation. Each student fills in their part of the missing dialogue.

- The dialogues can focus on any issue.

- The roles are then reversed so that both students have an opportunity to apply and adapt their knowledge of contextual talk to different situations.

Variations

- Dialogues can be carried out using the chat window function.

- Each pair could complete one section of the dialogue and then send it on to another pair in the class to complete the next section of the dialogue. Other pairs round-robin their completed dialogue sections as well.

- To extend this activity, the dialogues could be pasted into a Web page, and students could discuss the verbal modifications (linguistic and strategic adjustments) that they made to manage the context of the dialogue.

- Rather than having the entire dialogue written out, the teacher could supply a dialogue consisting of cues.

- As an extension, the teacher could put the role-play dialogues into a PowerPoint presentation and add sound files to the conversation. Alternatively, the students could make sound files of their half of the conversation as homework and e-mail them to the teacher for review.

Activity 13: Putting It Back Together

- Technology resources: Classroom with one or more computers or computer lab
- Technology type: Microsoft Word, chat, e-mail, video clips
- Nature of the activity: Conversing
- Task type: Information gap
- Proficiency level: Any
- Preparation and resources: A newspaper article
- Time: 15 minutes
- Participant structure: Individual or whole class
- Learning-how-to-learn skill: Responding to cues, filling in the blanks

Procedure

- This is an imaginative information gap activity that requires students to work in pairs or a group of students to act in unison and interact with another group of students at another site. A newspaper article is divided into its discrete components on separate pieces of paper. The pieces of paper are mixed and then divided into two parts. Part A is typed into a Word document, as is Part B (this can be done online by going to an online newspaper and then copying and pasting into a Word document).

- Part A is e-mailed to one student in a pair or to one group, and Part B is sent to another group.

- The object of the lesson is for students to rebuild—through chat or a group discussion board—the article into a logically sequenced whole.

Variations

- The negotiation between groups can take place through e-mail.

- Rather than using the components of a completed article, the teacher may want to use a video of a movie or news report from CNN. Students receive an edited version of a video clip.

Activity 14: Flow-On Creationism

- Technology resources: Classroom with one or more computers or computer lab

- Technology type: Microsoft Word, chat, e-mail, video clips

- Nature of the activity: Brainstorming

- Task type: Round-robin

- Proficiency level: Any

- Preparation and resources: None

- Time: 20 minutes

- Participant structure: Individual or group

- Learning-how-to-learn skill: Responding to cues

Procedure

- A list of visual cues is imported into a teacher-created Web page. The cues are pictures of various household objects, such as a microwave oven, a toy, a sound system, a table, and so on.

- Each group of students chooses one object from the list and creates a PowerPoint. presentations that is an instruction manual for how to put the object together.

- Each group creates a description of the item and includes that in the PowerPoint presentation. One member of the group types the description next to the cue, saves the document, and sends it to the next group as an e-mail attachment.

- Each group passes on their PowerPoint document once they have filled in a description of the object. The next group continues adding the assembly instructions. Once an instruction is added, the document is passed on. The trick is that the preceding group's input frames what the next group will write.

- Ultimately, the same number of instruction manuals will be created as their are groups in the class.

- Each manual can be pasted onto the teacher's Web site for the class to discuss.

Activity 15: Pick and Search

- Technology resources: Classroom with one or more computers or computer lab

- Technology type: Internet, Web page, LCD projector

- Nature of the activity: Listening and summarizing

- Task type: Reinforcing language and content knowledge

- Proficiency level: Intermediate to advanced

- Preparation and resources: None

- Time: 20 minutes

- Participant structure: Individual

- Learning-how-to-learn skill: Improvising and transferring knowledge

Procedure

- This activity is designed to confront students with different things that they must read, summarize, listen to, and retell. On his or her Web page, the teacher writes about cultural items, issues, and themes and displays the Web page through an LCD projector on a whiteboard. For example, the teacher may write about gothic architecture in France, the Holy Roman Empire, Barcelona, making sake, Buddhism, etc.

- Students are asked to pick a topic. Students have 20 minutes to surf the Internet, research the topic, and plan a five-minute lesson to teach the class about the topic.

- As the first student plans his or her five-minute lesson in a Microsoft Word document (so that it can be pasted onto the teacher's Web page), the teacher asks other students to pick an item.

- Once all of the students have picked an item, the students are given another five minutes to plan their presentation. The first student e-mails the information to the teacher, who pastes it onto the Web page, and explains what he or she has planned.

- After the presentation, the teacher and class have opportunity to provide constructive feedback.

Variations

♦ Rather than instructing students to provide constructive feedback after each presentation, the class is directed to provide synchronous feedback on the chat window while each student is giving his or her presentation.

♦ Presentations that are pasted on the Web page provide stimuli for students to highlight aspects of the cultural theme or ask questions about it. Groups or individuals are recognized by using different colored fonts.

Activity 16: Who's Who

♦ Technology resources: Classroom with one or more computers or computer lab

♦ Technology type: Internet, Web page, LCD projector

♦ Nature of the activity: Competition

♦ Task type: Language reinforcement

♦ Proficiency level: Intermediate to advanced

♦ Preparation and resources: Searching the Web

♦ Time: 20 minutes

♦ Participant structure: Individual

♦ Learning-how-to-learn skill: Researching and compiling information

Procedure

♦ The students' task is to search the Web for information about a well-known personality (perhaps culturally specific) and take notes on that person.

♦ Each student writes 10 facts about the person. The first few facts should be general and then become more detailed. The aim of the task is for the class to guess who the person is.

♦ If the class guesses after the first clue, they get 10 points; if they guess after the next clue, they get 9 points, and so on. The one with the most points wins.

♦ While the students are creating their clues, the teacher should write on the whiteboard the structures or particular language functions being studied at the time, which students should incorporate into their clues.

Variations

♦ Use the chat window function exclusively.

Activity 17: Wonderword Maze

- ♦ Technology resources: Classroom with one or more computers or computer lab

- ♦ Technology type: Internet, Web page, LCD projector

- ♦ Nature of the activity: Puzzle

- ♦ Task type: Language reinforcement

- ♦ Proficiency level: Any

- ♦ Preparation and resources: Creating a wonderword maze

- ♦ Time: 1 minute

- ♦ Participant structure: Individual

- ♦ Learning-how-to-learn skill: Spelling

Procedure

- ♦ The teacher pastes a wonderword maze created using an interactive online activity maker, such as Hot Potatoes or Quia. The puzzle is pasted into a Microsoft Word document and projected onto the classroom whiteboard.

- ♦ Students (identified by different colored markers) are asked to find as many words as they can. The student who find the most words wins.

Variations

- ♦ The wonderword maze can incorporate words specific to any curriculum area or topic.

- ♦ Students can be asked to create their own wonderword maze using words related to a specific topic.

Activity 18: Debate

- ♦ Technology resources: Classroom with one or more computers or computer lab

- ♦ Technology type: Internet, microphone, speakers

- ♦ Nature of the activity: Debate

- ♦ Task type: Language reinforcement

- ♦ Proficiency level: Any

- ♦ Preparation and resources: Listing debate topics

- ♦ Time: 20 minutes

- Participant structure: Group

- Learning-how-to-learn skill: Arguing a case, counterarguing, expressing opinions

Procedure

- The debate can take place between groups of people at different sites or between individuals at the same site. The topic can be chosen by the teacher or the students. For example, students search the Internet to find a current controversial issue related to education. The teacher can work with a teacher of another class or another school to hold a debate over the Internet using the Yahoo! audio chat function. Because the students may not be able to see one another, rules must be in place so that the debate runs smoothly: the parameters of the debate, the number of students on each side, the length, the criteria for judging, the language forms to be used, etc.

- The teacher or a student adjudicates.

Variations

- The teacher instruct students to conduct the same debate once again, though this time through the chat window function. By doing so, students can extend their arguments and incorporate constructive feedback received from the teacher and fellow students.

- A number of debates may be carried on at the same time. Divide the class into four groups. Two groups argue the affirmative side, and two groups argue the negative side. If there are more than three students in a group (first, second, and third speaker), the other students may act as secretaries or researchers, or they may provide constructive feedback to each speaker. Once the sides have chosen, the teacher writes the topic on the whiteboard. The first group of debaters interacts using the audio function, while the other group uses the chat window function. The teacher can listen to and read each debate as it is happening.

Activity 19: Building Blocks

- Technology resources: Classroom with one or more computers or computer lab

- Technology type: Internet, microphone, speakers, chat, or e-mail

- Nature of the activity: Metacommunication

- Task type: Using directives

- Proficiency level: Intermediate

- Preparation and resources: Building blocks

- ◆ Time: 20 minutes

- ◆ Participant structure: Pairs

- ◆ Learning-how-to-learn skill: Giving instructions

Procedure

- ◆ Part of a teacher's job is to communicate clearly and concisely and to provide feedback and encourage students to question and participate in classroom discussions. This activity gives students an opportunity to use language to describe a process and to instruct other people to carry out an action. For this activity, students need to work in pairs and use chat. The teacher will have delivered to everyone the same type and amount of building materials.

- ◆ Student A in each pair builds something with the building blocks provided. When Student A is finished, he or she tells Student B how to make the same construction. Student B follows the instructions (using the same materials and making it in the same way).

- ◆ Because there will be many pairs if the class is large, it is advisable for interaction to take place through a number of media (some may use the audio function, some may use the chat window function, while others use e-mail).

Variation

- ◆ To make the activity more demanding, use different colored building blocks. If cameras are available, the groups can show their constructions and compare them.

Activity 20: "Guess What" Free-for-All

- ◆ Technology resources: Classroom with one or more computers or computer lab

- ◆ Technology type: Chat or e-mail

- ◆ Nature of the activity: Using language to describe

- ◆ Task type: Listening comprehension

- ◆ Proficiency level: Intermediate

- ◆ Preparation and resources: None

- ◆ Time: 20 minutes

- ◆ Participant structure: Whole class

- ◆ Learning-how-to-learn skill: Decoding and encoding

Procedure

♦ The students are asked to think of an object in their home or classroom. They write down four statements about the object. The statements should be based on the language structures learned in class.

♦ In turn, each student writes out his or her first statement in the chat window. If another student knows what the object is, he or she types it on the chat. If not, the student write out his or her second statement, and so on.

♦ Once someone has guessed the object, there is a teacher-lead discussion about what the other students thought the object was and why.

Variation

♦ Rather than have the guessing go on simultaneously, students communicate their statements in turn and continue to do so until someone guesses the object. The lesson continues as other students write out their statements.

Activity 21: When Can I Butt In?

♦ Technology resources: Classroom with one or more computers or computer lab

♦ Technology type: Chat, e-mail, or audio

♦ Nature of the activity: Asking questions, language enhancement

♦ Task type: Information gap

♦ Proficiency level: Intermediate

♦ Preparation and resources: None

♦ Time: 15 minutes

♦ Participant structure: Whole class

♦ Learning-how-to-learn skill: Managing technology and establishing routines

Procedure

♦ This is a game that checks students' understanding of a particular function. Each student is given the name of a person, real or imaginary. The students' task is to guess who the person is by asking questions of the class. Student will receive an e-mail through Nicenet telling them who everyone else is except themselves.

♦ Every student must try to find out who they are. However, they can do so only by asking yes/no questions.

- Students can ask questions through any function that the computer allows (audio, chat, e-mail); however, the class must establish routines and rules of communication so that every student does not use the same function and so that all students are not communicating at once.

- After establishing these rules, the class proceeds to find out who they are. The first person to guess wins.

- The important aspect of this activity is not the guessing but the interaction among the students to establish the rules of communication and turn taking.

Activity 22: Interrogation

- Technology resources: Classroom with one or more computers or computer lab

- Technology type: Chat, audio, Microsoft PowerPoint

- Nature of the activity: Asking questions, language enhancement

- Task type: Puzzle

- Proficiency level: Intermediate

- Preparation and resources: None

- Time: 15 minutes

- Participant structure: Individual or pair

- Learning-how-to-learn skill: Asking questions to elicit information

Procedure

- This activity requires students to practice asking a variety of questions. The teacher gives the class a story (if it is a story that the students know, the teacher only provides the title; if it is an unknown story, the teacher first reads the story to the class). Rather than simply reading the story, the teacher has already recorded the story on a sound file and made a PowerPoint presentation. In other words, the PowerPoint becomes an audio-visual "big book." The PowerPoint presentation is added to the teacher's Web page so that students who do not finish the task can do so at home.

- When each student fully understands the content of the story, the teacher directs individuals or pairs to write down as many questions as they can. After a fixed amount of time, the individual or pair with the most questions or greatest variety of questions wins.

Variations

♦ The story can be an article, a newspaper clip, or any other artifact. Students are guided to focus on topics in their area (or any other area).

♦ If students are given the same piece of writing, they can type their questions into the chat window. When the teacher says "Stop," they must quickly press enter so that their words come up on the chat window. The first set of questions to appear wins.

Activity 23: Lesson Comics

♦ Technology resources: Classroom with one or more computers or computer lab

♦ Technology type: Chat, audio, Web page, video

♦ Nature of the activity: Negotiating

♦ Task type: Puzzle

♦ Proficiency level: Any

♦ Preparation and resources: Digital still photographs

♦ Time: 35 minutes

♦ Participant structure: Pair or group

♦ Learning-how-to-learn skill: Recognizing sequences

Procedure

♦ The teacher needs a digital camera. The aim is to take a series of snapshots of any process, such as preparing a dinner, going on holiday, shopping, or playing. The teacher should have at least 10 digital photos for this activity.

♦ The digital photos should numbered randomly and then imported into the teacher's Web page before the lesson. The logical sequence of the snapshots is mixed up.

♦ The object of this activity is for pairs or groups to discuss (in the target language) the correct sequence of the snapshots.

♦ Once completed, the students must justify their choices.

Variation

♦ This activity could be carried out as an information gap activity. The class is divided into pairs. Student A sees half of the pictures (on a Web page or in a Word document), and Student B receives the other half of the pictures. Each student must ask the other questions and describe his or her own set of pictures to the other before negotiating the sequence. Students can carry out this activity by writing in the chat window or e-mail.

♦ The digital shots could be a series of video clips with sound.

♦ The students could be asked to take a series of video clips of a process, add commentary, and then follow steps above.

Activity 24: You, Too, Can Teach in 10 Easy Steps

♦ Technology resources: Classroom with one or more computers or computer lab

♦ Technology type: Internet

♦ Nature of the activity: Organizing Students for a Online Quest

♦ Task type: Discovery

♦ Proficiency level: Intermediate

♦ Preparation and resources: Preparing an evaluation rubric

♦ Time: 15–35 minutes

♦ Participant structure: Individual, pair, or group

♦ Learning-how-to-learn skill: Searching and providing input

Procedure

♦ This activity helps students learn instructional strategies for directing others to follow a procedure or set of instructions. Students are first organized to work by themselves, either in pairs or in groups, depending on the student-to-computer ratio.

♦ The students surf the Internet to find an appropriate curriculum Web site with shareware or public domain facilities. The students find an activity that they will download (if necessary), explain it to the class, and organize the class to carry out the activity.

Variations

♦ The teacher may want to have students carry out this activity a number of times, introducing conditions that make the organization of the class progressively more complicated. For example, in the first round, students might be instructed to find a whole-class activity, explain the activity, and operationalize it. Next, the teacher might instructs students to find a group and then a pair activity. Next, students must find an activity that must be explained and operationalized using the audio function of the computer (in other words, a listening activity), then using the chat window function, then e-mail, the Internet, and Microsoft PowerPoint. In this way, students learn how to find foreign language activities that suit different environments and modes of operationalization and how to learn a foreign language by doing a range of online activities. This activity allows the class to build up a bank of reusable activities.

♦ The students can share their activities and rate them. The teacher can go to any of the online rubric template Web sites, prepare a rating rubric, have the students do the activities or games, and rate them.

Activity 25: That's Entertainment

♦ Technology resources: Classroom with one or more computers or computer lab

♦ Technology type: Chat, LCD projector

♦ Nature of the activity: Discussion

♦ Task type: Game

♦ Proficiency level: Any

♦ Preparation and resources: None

♦ Time: 15–35 minutes

♦ Participant structure: Individual, pair, or group

♦ Learning-how-to-learn skill: Justifying opinions

Procedure

♦ The teacher asks each student to think of 10 movies. This is good practice for *katakana* (Japanese) or any other non–Western script language. A Microsoft Word document is opened and projected onto the board, and students write down the movies they have listed.

♦ Students put a check mark next to every movie they have seen. For each check mark, that student gets one point. The student with the most point wins.

♦ Next, the teacher leads an online discussion (using a discussion board, chat, or e-mail) about the movies the students have seen (plot, characters, good and bad points). Students explain their opinions.

Activity 26: Tell Me Lies, Tell Me Sweet Little Lies

- ♦ Technology resources: Classroom with one or more computers or computer lab

- ♦ Technology type: Chat, LCD projector

- ♦ Nature of the activity: Listening for understanding

- ♦ Task type: Information gap

- ♦ Proficiency level: Any

- ♦ Preparation and resources: None

- ♦ Time: 20 minutes

- ♦ Participant structure: Individual, pair, or group

- ♦ Learning-how-to-learn skill: Filling in the blanks

Procedure

- ♦ The teacher recalls a recent event that happened in the classroom and recounts it in the form of a story—recorded on a sound file (or split into many sound files and made into a PowerPoint presentation). The teacher tells the story from the students' point of view but adds some elements. After listening to the story and taking notes, the students must decide what was left out, what was added, and how the experience was different for them.

- ♦ The students' answers are recorded in a Word document and displayed on the board. Students write their opinions beneath these responses. A teacher-led discussion about the students' opinions takes place. Mistakes on the whiteboard are corrected.

Variations

- ♦ As the teacher relates the story, the students write down what the teachers says, correcting the story as it is told.

- ♦ As students listen to sound files of the story, they signify the first time the teacher relates an event that did not occur. The first student to first pick up the discrepancy continues to tell the story using the chat window function. When this student writes something that is untrue, the student who notices picks up the narration, also using the chat window function. The activity continues until the event has been retold in its entirety and in a way that everyone agrees on.

Activity 27: What Does It Mean?

- ◆ Technology resources: Classroom with one or more computers or computer lab
- ◆ Technology type: Chat
- ◆ Nature of the activity: Practicing language
- ◆ Task type: Puzzle
- ◆ Proficiency level: Any
- ◆ Preparation and resources: None
- ◆ Time: 10 minutes
- ◆ Participant structure: Individual
- ◆ Learning-how-to-learn skill: Using language functions creatively

Procedure

- ◆ The teacher writes 10 letters in the chat window or on the whiteboard. The students must look at the letters, say a word that begins with each letter, and then make a sentence out of these words. For example, M R U T T C A F N S T I: Mary ran under the tunnel carefully as Frank nicely slipped through it.

- ◆ If the letters are too difficult to make a sentence with (and depending on the proficiency level of the students), the class could create a rule, such as "up to two letters can be changed." The sentences are written up on the whiteboard.

Activity 28: In the Know

- ◆ Technology resources: Classroom with one or more computers or computer lab
- ◆ Technology type: Internet, Microsoft PowerPoint
- ◆ Nature of the activity: Practicing language structures
- ◆ Task type: Inquiry learning
- ◆ Proficiency level: Intermediate to advanced
- ◆ Preparation and resources: None
- ◆ Time: 30 minutes to one week
- ◆ Participant structure: Individual
- ◆ Learning-how-to-learn skill: Researching

Procedure

◆ Students become motivated when they have an opportunity to interact with people outside the classroom (other than their peers or teacher). This activity requires students to look up a person in another country (e.g., Spain, Austria, Switzerland, Japan, China), interact them by e-mail, and find out about a recent event in that country.

◆ This information is compiled and written down in a Word document and sent to another student in the class.

◆ The teacher decides who will send their reports whom to ensure that one student doesn't receive multiple reports. The student who receives the report edits it and sends it to a third person, who reads the final draft. The third person may ask author or the editor questions using e-mail or chat.

◆ Once the third student is satisfied, he or she presents the report to the class.

◆ As the teacher listens to each report, effective structures and functions are written on a whiteboard. This way, students learn language and culturally specific information from their peers.

Variation

◆ The students compile the information and make a PowerPoint book or a Web collage.

Activity 29: A Wrinkle in Time

◆ Technology resources: Classroom with one or more computers or computer lab

◆ Technology type: Internet, Microsoft PowerPoint, chat

◆ Nature of the activity: Practicing language structures

◆ Task type: Inquiry learning

◆ Proficiency level: Intermediate to advanced

◆ Preparation and resources: None

◆ Time: 30 minutes to one week

◆ Participant structure: Individual

◆ Learning-how-to-learn skill: Researching

Procedure

♦ This activity is designed to find out "how" other students are: How they learn in their classes, how they are motivated, how they communicate effectively, how they manage their work, and how they plan for successful learning. The teacher posts 10 questions on his or her Web page. These questions will frame the activity and guide the students in thinking about "how" students are in other countries and "how" they were in the past or will be in the future. The teacher tells the students to imagine they have a time machine and can travel to different times in the past and future in other countries. While there, the students ask questions such as

- You are in 19th-century France—what is your school like?

- What is it like at school in Germany during World War II?

- What is your teacher like during the 1960s in Spain?

- What courses do you take as a student in 20th-century Mexico?

- Do you have the opportunity to go to a university in 18th-century Japan?

- When and where do such institutions exist?

- What is it like to have a governess in the 19th century?

- How is a Latin American student of the 21st century different from students of the past?

♦ Students then write a story using the language structures they have learned in class and relying on what they know about being a student. They apply this knowledge to analyze how each student works, how students worked in the past, and what educational approaches to learning they use.

♦ These stories are sent to the teacher. Mistakes are corrected by the students, and each story is posted in subsequent lessons on the teacher's Web page for the class to deconstruct (this may occur through the chat window function).

Activity 30: Discovery Questioning

♦ Technology resources: Classroom with one or more computers or computer lab

♦ Technology type: Internet, Microsoft PowerPoint, chat, e-mail, Web page

♦ Nature of the activity: Practicing language structures

♦ Task type: Inquiry learning

- ♦ Proficiency level: Intermediate to advanced

- ♦ Preparation and resources: Finding online detective stories

- ♦ Time: 15 minutes to one week

- ♦ Participant structure: Individual

- ♦ Learning-how-to-learn skill: Making deductions

Procedure

- ♦ The teacher finds a range of short detective stories (as many stories as there are students in the class).

- ♦ The teacher types the stories into a Microsoft Word document and e-mails them to the students, posts them on the teacher's Web page (with a hotlink), or rewrites them to the level of the students in PowerPoint.

- ♦ The students are instructed to open their story and read it through. The teacher divides the class into pairs. The aim of the activity is for students to learn the plot and "whodunit" of the story by asking yes/no questions. However, instead of orally asking questions, Student A in each pair asks questions using e-mail or chat. When the story has been discovered, student B writes (e-mail or chat) to Student A.

Activity 31: A Wrinkle in Time II

- ♦ Technology resources: Classroom with one or more computers or computer lab

- ♦ Technology type: Internet, chat, e-mail

- ♦ Nature of the activity: Practicing language structures

- ♦ Task type: Inquiry reading

- ♦ Proficiency level: Intermediate to advanced

- ♦ Preparation and resources: Online newspapers

- ♦ Time: 30 minutes to one week

- ♦ Participant structure: Group or whole class

- ♦ Learning-how-to-learn skill: Comprehending through context

Procedure

- ♦ This activity is an ongoing project for the whole term, although initially, the teacher may want to spend 30 minutes or a whole lesson on the activity.

- The teacher breaks the class into groups (as many groups as there are computer terminals). To facilitate written discourse in the classroom, it is preferable for members of each group to be drawn together through writing or by using the chat window or e-mail. Each group is asked to find an article on a particular topic (searching the Web is an easy way to access articles, newspaper clippings, or other information about a particular topic).

- Once each group has found an article, they are instructed to make a chart with three columns: "Words and Phrases I Know," "Words and Phrases I Am Familiar With but Can't Readily Identify," and "Words and Phrases I Don't Know."

- Each student in the group reads the article and fills in the three columns.

- Once this is completed, the group comes back together and discusses (through chat or e-mail, as directed by the teacher) what each student filled in. The aim of the exercise is for students to share their knowledge about words and phrases they know and to find out more about words and phrases they are familiar with but can't readily identify. The teacher can use the students list of "Words and Phrases I Don't Know" as a homework dictionary exercise or as a follow-up activity using an online activity builder such as Hot Potatoes or Quia.

Activity 32: WebQuesting

- Technology type: Internet

- Nature of the activity: Higher-order thinking

- Task type: Discovery learning

- Proficiency level: Beginner, intermediate, or advanced

- Time: 30 minutes to one week

- Learning-how-to-learn skill: Comprehending through context, research skills

Procedure

- A WebQuest is an inquiry-based activity that requires students to search specific Web sites for information to complete a predetermined task. The WebQuest has six components: (1) an engaging opening, (2) a question or task, (3) background information, (4) specific Web sites, (5) real-world feedback in terms of a rubric, and (6) a conclusion.

- To become familiar with the format and range of WebQuests, we recommend that looking at the following Web sites in the order they are given here:

  - Definitions and explanations
    http://edweb.sdsu.edu/courses/edtec596/about_WebQuests.html

- Building blocks of a WebQuest:
  http://projects.edtech.sandi.net/staffdev/buildingblocks/p_index.htm

- WebQuest workshop:
  http://www.thirtenn.org/edonline/concept2class/WebQuests/index.html

- WebQuest about WebQuests:
  http://WebQuest.sdsu.edu/WebQuestWebQuest-hs.html

- WebQuest template:
  http://WebQuest.sdsu.edu/designpatterns/COMM/WebQuest.htm

- WebQuest design patterns:
  http://WebQuest.sdsu.edu/designpatterns/all.htm

- Process checklist:
  http://WebQuest.sdsu.edu/processchecker.html

- WebQuest patterns:
  http://projects.edtech.sandi.net/staffdevtpss98/patterns-taxonomy.html

- WebQuest Task Types:
  http://WebQuest.sdsu.edu/taskonomy.html

♦ Now try to build your own…your imagination is your only limitation. If you want to brush up on your own Spanish or foreign language methodological skills, we have created some WebQuests for you at http://seeds.coedu.usf.edu/spanishEnhance/WebQuests/questmain/WebQuests_main.html.

References

Beauvois, M.H. (1992). Computer-assisted classroom discussion in the foreign language classroom: Conversation in slow motion. *Foreign Language Annals, 25*(5), 455–463.

Bradley, T., & Lomika, L. (2000). A case study of learner interaction in technology-enhanced language learning environments. *Journal of Educational Computing Research, 22*(3), 347–368.

Chun, D.M. (1994). Using computer networking to facilitate the acquisition of interactive competence. *System, 22*(1), 17–31.

Cubillos, J.H. (1998). Technology: A step forward in the teaching of foreign languages. In J. Harper, M. Lively, & M. Williams (Eds.), *The coming of age of the profession: Issues and emerging ideas for the teaching of foreign languages* (pp. 37–52). Boston: Heinle & Heinle.

Gonglewski, M.R. (1999). Linking the Internet to the national standards for foreign language learning. *Foreign Language Annals, 32,* 348–362.

Gonzalez-Edflet, N. (1990). Oral interaction and collaboration at the computer: Learning English as a second language with the help of your peers. *Computers in the Schools, 7*(1–2), 53–90.

Keen, R.G. (1995). Restructuring classroom interaction with networked computers: Effects on quantity and characteristics of language production. *The Modern Language Journal, 79*(4), 457–476.

Kelm, O.R. (1992). The use of synchronous computer networks in second language instruction: A preliminary report. *Foreign Language Annals, 25*(5), 441–453.

Salaberry, M. (1996). A theoretical foundation for the development of pedagogical tasks in computer mediated communication. *CALICO Journal, 14*(1) 5–36.

Sotillo, S.M. (2000). Discourse functions and syntactic complexity in synchronous and asynchronous communication. *Language Learning & Technology, 4*(1), 82–119.

Warshauer, M. (1996). Comparing face-to-face and electronic discussion in the second language classroom. *CALICO Journal, 13*(2), 7–26.

18
Gates in Cyberland

Annmarie Zoran

A variety of technological tools and their applications have been presented in this book. We hope that the activities presented here will provide further ideas and open the "gates" for the diverse use of these applications in your foreign language classroom.

It is fitting that this book conclude with additional resources for gateway and specialized sites for foreign language teaching. What are gateway sites? Generally speaking, they are Web sites that provide a bank of resources on a specific subject. The gateway sites presented here have been used, tested, and recommended by foreign language educators. These sites are not search engines but rather gates to excellent resources within the field of foreign and second language learning. They are Web sites that bank, evaluate, or collect resources for foreign language educators. This chapter also presents selected specialized Web sites for different foreign languages.

Finally, a variety of applications and tools are listed here, some of which have been discussed in the previous chapters, and others that you can try out with or for your students. They are teacher-friendly applications that are highly recommended.

It is our aim that these resources complement the resources that are already in your library—that they will assist you in "CALLing" learners toward authentic and meaningful foreign language education.

Gateway Sites

Globe-Gate CALL Research Center

http://globegate.utm.edu/french/ globegate_mirror/call.html

♦ This site, created and maintained by "Tennessee Bob" (a.k.a. Robert Peckham), offers a wealth of resources and excellent links to articles, lesson plans, activities, and professional organizations. The resources are divided into the following topics:

- Technology-assisted language learning bibliographies

- CALL journals and newsletters

- Language learning software

- CALL organizations and institutions

- Computers and language learning (includes links about e-pals, the effectiveness of multimedia, considerations in implementing a computer lab, and help topics for Macs and PCs)

- Internet and language learning (MOOs, courseware tools, Web projects, Internet tools)

- Distance learning and foreign language education

- Computer processing language

Multimedia Educational Resource for Learning and Online Teaching (MERLOT)

http://www.merlot.org/Home.po

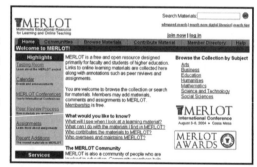

◆ MERLOT is a free and open resource with links to online learning. All of the online learning materials go through a peer review process. This site also provides a search function to quickly find resources.

Foreign Language Lessons Plans and Resources for Teachers

http://www.csun.edu/~hcedu013/eslsp.html

◆ A collection of links to lesson plans, activities, resources, and museum links for Spanish, French, German, Japanese, Chinese, Latin, and other languages.

Center for Advanced Research on Language Acquisition (CARLA)

http://www.carla.umn.edu/index.html

◆ Sponsored by the U.S. Department of Education's Title VI Language Resource Center, CARLA engages in a number of research projects, such as content-based language teaching through technology (http://www.carla.umn.edu/cobaltt/), culture and language learning (http://www.carla.umn.edu/culture/), immersion education and research (http://www.carla.umn.edu/immersion/), less commonly taught languages (http://www.carla.umn.edu/lctl/), pragmatics and speech acts (http://www.carla.umn.edu/speechacts/), second language assessment (http://www.carla.umn.edu/assessment/), second language learning strategies (http://www.carla.umn.edu/strategies/), and technology and language learning (http://www.carla.umn.edu/technology/). This gateway sites offers a vast array of resources for language teachers, including professional development opportunities, strategies, suggestions, and current publications.

FL Teach (Foreign Language Teaching Forum)

http://www.cortland.edu/flteach/flteach-res.html

♦ This site is a collection of Web resources recommended by foreign language teachers. Its resources include media, collections made by teachers for teachers, adolescents, general foreign language resources, online journals, favorite foreign language resources, and language-specific sites for Chinese, French, German, Italian, Latin, Portuguese, Russian, and Spanish.

Language Links

http://polyglot.lss.wisc.edu/lss/lang/langlink.html

♦ Language Links provides ideas for integrating the World Wide Web into the classroom, with additional resources on multilingualism, African languages and literature, Asian studies, classics, English as a second language, French, Germanic languages, Hebrew and Semitic studies, Italian, Portuguese, Quechua, Scandinavian studies, Slavic languages, and Spanish.

E. L. Easton Languages Online

http://eleaston.com/languages.html

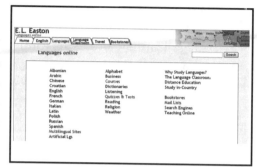

♦ This site provides a springboard for re-sources on a variety of languages (Albanian, Arabic, Chinese, Croatian, English, French, German, Italian, Latin, Polish, Russian, Spanish, multilingual sites). It also includes dictionaries, language skills, religion, weather, and assessments.

Foreign Language Resources

http://webgerman.com/languages/

♦ This site offers links and resources for American Sign Language, Arabic, Baltic, Basque, Chinese, Dutch, Danish, Finnish, French, German, Gaelic, Hawaiian, Hebrew, Italian, Japanese, Persian, Polish, Portuguese, Russian, Serbo-Croatian, Slavic, Slovenian, Samoan, Sanskrit, Spanish, Swahili, Swedish, Tagalog, Thai, Turkish, and Yiddish. The site also provides links to live audio and video; quick phrases; holiday activities in German, French, Spanish, and English; and a multilanguage reference resource guide.

Educator's Reference Desk

http://www.eduref.org/cgi-bin/lessons.cgi/Foreign_Language

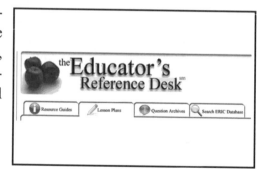

♦ This site features unique lesson plans submitted by teachers. Sample lesson plans are available for Chinese, French, Spanish, American Sign Language, English as a second language, linguistics, and cultural awareness.

Web-Based Activities for Foreign Languages

http://facweb.furman.edu/~pecoy/lessons.htm

♦ This Web site offers mostly French activities, but is a good showcase of how teachers can make their exercises interactive. The topics include grammar, vocabulary, listening comprehension, information discovery, Web-based activities, and other multimedia uses of the Web.

Foreign Languages Besides English on the Web

http://www.geocities.com/vance_stevens//for_lang.htm

♦ This site, created by Vance Stevens, includes information specific to Arabic, Chinese, Dutch, French, German, Greek, Japanese, Malay, Portuguese, Russian, and Spanish speakers. It provides common foreign language resources, newspapers, and translation services.

VCU Trail Guide to International Sites and Language Resources

http://www.fln.vcu.edu/default.html

♦ This site is a list of resources and links for French, German, Italian, Spanish, and Russian created by Virginia Commonwealth University.

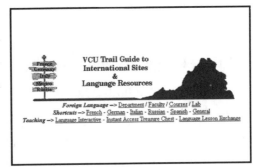

Internet Resources for Language Teachers and Learners

http://www.fredriley.org.uk/call/langsite/

♦ This is a gateway for language teachers that includes general links (linguistics, newspapers and periodicals, organizations, software) and links to language-specific sites (Balkan languages, Celtic languages, Eastern European languages, TEFL/TESL, French, German, Hispanic languages, Italian, Indian, Dutch, Middle Eastern languages, Oriental languages, Portuguese, Scandinavian languages), multilingual sites, Internet-based learning sites, search engines, and commercial sites.

Foreign Language and Culture

http://www.speakeasy.org/~dbrick/Hot/foreign.html

♦ The Foreign Language and Culture page offers easy access to hundreds of language-related sites.

Internet Activities for Foreign Language Classrooms

http://www.clta.net/lessons/

Internet Activities for Foreign Language Classes

♦ This Web site provides basic information on how to write activities for the Web, considerations that need to be taken into account, reading strategies, and Web evaluations. The site provides resources for different proficiency levels of Spanish, French, German, Chinese, Japanese, Italian, Tagalog, and Latin.

UCLA Language Materials Project

http://www.lmp.ucla.edu/

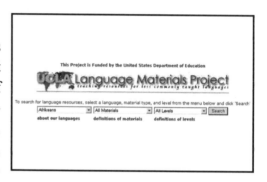

♦ Hosted by the University of California, Los Angeles, and funded by the U.S. Department of Education, this site provides a database of more than 900 languages and 11,000 citations. The database offers linguistic profiles, geographic distributions of languages, grammatical features, historical background, and key dialects.

Foreign Language Videos

http://worlddmc.ohiolink.edu/Language/Login

♦ Created by the OhioLINK Digital Media Center, this site provides a collection of foreign language video clips in Arabic (classical), Chinese (Mandarin), French, German, Russian, Spanish, and Swahili pertaining to culture, family, daily life, and more. Each video clip includes a description of its content, the country of the speaker, and additional grammar and vocabulary notes.

Specialized Web Sites

German

German Resources on the Web

http://grow.aatg.org/

♦ German Resources on the Web, created by the American Association of Teachers of German, includes links to Web resources, Web activities, Web exercises, standards-based thematic units, projects, and an online course. Instructors are encouraged to submit their resources.

The German Way

http://www.german-way.com

♦ Developed by the author of *The German Way*, this site provides resources on teaching; cultural topics; famous Austrians, Germans, and Swiss; foreign language organizations online; genealogy links; information and photos by country; and Web links for teachers.

Learn German Online

http://www.learn-german-online.net/

♦ This site is an online resource for learning German as a foreign language, textbooks, learning software, dictionaries, tests, German culture and literature, cinema, culture, television and radio, public festivals, museums, and practical guides and tips.

German for Travelers

http://www.germanfortravellers.com/

♦ Initially created as German for Beginners by Dr. Peter Golz, this site has expanded to German for Travellers, a free resource with instructional materials, learning exercises, online courses, and hotlinks.

French

American Association of Teachers of French

http://www.frenchteachers.org/technology/

♦ Hosted by the main French professional teaching organization in the United States, this site provides a multitude of resources on technology, software, computer-aided language learning, pedagogical applications (a must see!), copyright rules, and position papers. It also offer a search function.

Tennessee Bob's Famous French Links

http://www.utm.edu/departments/french/french.html

♦ A part of the Globe-Gate supersite (see the previous section in this chapter), Tennessee Bob's Famous French Links provides a wealth of resources and has received a five-star rating from MERLOT.

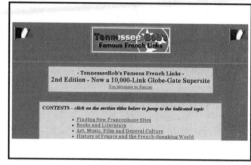

Japanese

Japanese Language Learning Tools on the Web

http://www.sabotenweb.com/bookmarks/language.html

♦ Created by Keiko Schneider, this site provides a list of resources ranging from dictionaries to online Japanese tutoring, survival Japanese, reference materials, translation sites, teaching your children Japanese, language proficiency tests, and online courses.

Japanese Online

http://www.japanese-online.com/

♦ This Web site offers a free online dictionary, lessons, discussion forum, and useful links for learning Japanese.

Japanese Online Resources

http://hcl.harvard.edu/harvard-yenching/japandatabase.html

♦ This site is a digital resource guide for Japanese studies that includes general resources such as library catalogs, lists of book vendors, periodicals indexes, newspapers, dictionaries, maps. Resources by subject cover anthropology; art, film, and culture; East Asian studies; economics and finance; history; law; literature; politics and government; religion; sociology; statistics; and other Japanese studies sites.

Latin

VRoma

http://www.vroma.org/course_materials/

♦ VRoma is a community of teacher and student scholars who create online resources for teaching Latin and ancient Roman culture. The resources topics cover the Latin language, texts and authors, history and culture, using the VRoma MOO for teaching, and sample class assignments in the VRoma MOO.

Intermediate Latin Readings

http://www.iona.edu/latin/

♦ An online supplement for intermediate-level Latin, this Web site offers 12 texts by four authors with assisted glosses. Students may read, download, and print the text and send translations to their professors for grading. This program also offers a comment/question box, a resource section, and a list of classical sites.

Latin Dictionary and Grammar Aid

http://www.nd.edu/~archives/latgramm.htm

♦ Developed and adapted by Kevin Crawley of the University of Notre Dame, this site allows users to type in a stem or ending and receive an English dictionary translation.

Russian

Online Russian Language Center

http://learningrussian.com/

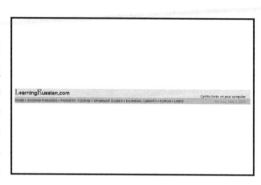

♦ This online center provides educational resources on learning Russian as a foreign language at all levels and offers both a free and a premium service. Resources include reference guides on personal and business correspondence; Russian names and holidays, the Russian alphabet and ;phonetic system; and Russian nouns, adjectives, pronouns, numerals, and verbs. It also features a reading room with online library, proverbs and sayings, bilingual comics, online dictionaries, newsletters, discussion board, and links.

Russian Inter-Active Online Reference Grammar

http://www.departments.bucknell.edu/russian/language/

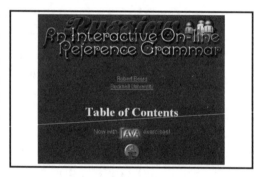

♦ This Web site provides a springboard of references such as Cyrillic fonts and keyboards; the Cyrillic alphabet; pronunciation; Russian verbs, nouns, adjectives, pronouns, prepositions, and conjunctions; and Russian dictionaries, reading texts, and online materials.

Russnet Language Modules

http://www.russnet.org/online.html

♦ This Web site offers free thematic modules for Russian-language instruction in RealPlayer format. Themes include business Russian, modules for high school to college education, and a cultural map of Russia.

Spanish

Support for Elementary Educators through Distance Educators in Spanish (SEEDS)

http://coedu.usf.edu

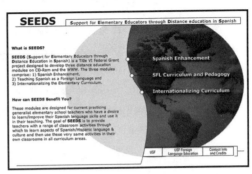

♦ SEEDS is designed for teachers who want to learn Spanish, teach Spanish, or internationalize their curriculum through content-based teaching. It contains hundreds of sequenced activities, WebQuests, and video clips of best practices. This site was developed by Tony Erben at the University of South Florida under a Title VI grant.

Del.iscio.us Social Bookmarking

http://del.icio.us/languagetechnology/Spanish

♦ Del.iscio.us is a Web site of links on the World Wide Web that have been collected and shared by individuals around the world. You can create your own favorites and bookmarks. More than 40 Spanish resources are currently offered.

BBC Languages: Spanish

http://www.bbc.co.uk/languages/spanish/index.shtml

♦ This Web site from the BBC in the United Kingdom offers online courses for beginners and intermediate learners. It also provides resources for tutors, an audio magazine, games and quizzes, and a feature section about the Spanish language.

WWW Virtual Library

http://www2.etown.edu/vl/forlange.html

♦ This gateway site offers resources divided by types of information, as well as language-, country- and place-specific searches.

Super Spanish Web Sites

http://www.uni.edu/becker/Spanish3.html

♦ Internet resources for testing your Spanish level, as well as grammar help, children's and games sites, colleges and universities, resources for learning Spanish abroad, and food and cuisine. The main page offers additional resources for French, Chinese, and Japanese.

Online Activities

Hot Potatoes

http://web.uvic.ca/hrd/halfbaked/sites6.htm

♦ This is a list of sites that have used the Hot Potatoes application to create foreign language activities. Many activities include video, audio, and images to enhance students' language learning. (See Chapter 14 in this book for more information on Hot Potatoes.)

WebQuest Page

http://webquest.sdsu.edu/

♦ The WebQuest Page provides an excellent overview of WebQuests, as well as examples and training materials.

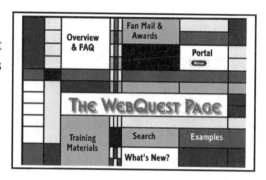

Online Applications: Tools for Teachers and Students

Nicenet

http://www.nicenet.org

♦ Nicenet is a free courseware tool that assists teachers with classroom management and communication. Nicenet provides functions for sharing or annotating links, posting documents, online conferencing, turning in assignments online, class scheduling and administration, and viewing and sending personal messages. It is a great resource for foreign language teachers to use with their students. (See Chapter 12 in this book for more information on integrating Nicenet into the classroom).

Hot Potatoes

http://web.uvic.ca/hrd/halfbaked/

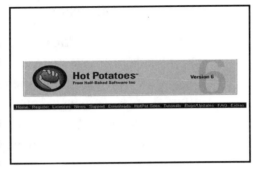

◆ Hot Potatoes is a downloadable application that allows teachers and students to create their own multiple-choice, short-answer, jumbled-sentence, crossword, matching-ordering, and gap-fill exercises for the Web. Hot Potatoes is free to those working in publicly funded nonprofit educational institutions. (See the "Specialized Web Sites" section in this chapter for a list of sites that use Hot Potatoes.)

McSkins

http://www.learnertools.com/mcskins/multiple_choice.html

◆ McSkins is a free Flash-based companion to the multiple-choice application available in Hot Potatoes. It allows teachers and students to create multiple-choice quizzes and reading activities on the Web.

CrossSkins

http://www.learnertools.com/crossskins/crossword.html

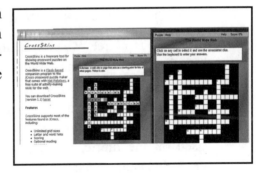

◆ CrossSkins is a free Flash-based companion to the JCross (crossword puzzle) application in Hot Potatoes. It allows teachers and students to create crossword puzzles on the Web.

4Teachers

http://www.4teachers.org/

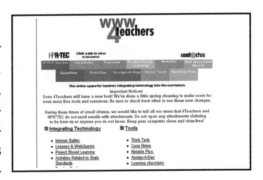

◆ This site offers free tools and resources for integrating technology into any classroom. It includes tools for taking notes (NoteStar), creating rubrics (RubriStar), creating quizzes (QuizStar), and organizing and annotating Web sites (TrackStar). It also provides links to professional development organizations and resources for integrating technology into the classroom.

NoteStar

http://notestar.4teachers.org/

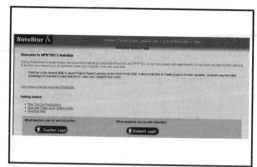

♦ NoteStar is a note taking tool for teachers and students. It allows students to create topics, assign topics to group members, track information, and organize notes and sources. Teachers can use NoteStar to create projects, track group progress, and manage multiple classes.

QuizStar

http://quizstar.4teachers.org/

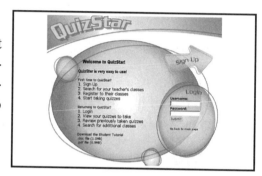

♦ QuizStar is a free Web-based program that allows instructors to create quizzes (including multilingual quizzes), use report management tools, and attach media files to quizzes.

RubriStar

http://rubistar.4teachers.org/index.php

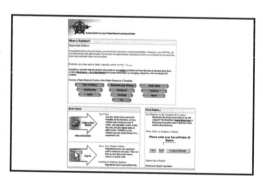

♦ RubriStar is a free Web-based application that allows instructors and students to generate rubrics. Categories are already written, or you can make changes to suit your needs. After students have completed projects based on the rubric, instructors can enter scores and analyze the results.

TrackStar

http://trackstar.hprtec.org/

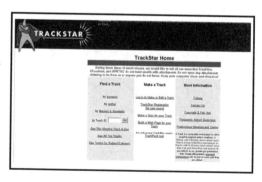

♦ This application allows teachers and students to annotate and organize Web sites for lessons or search existing annotated Web sites created by instructors.

Web Worksheet Wizard

http://wizard.hprtec.org/

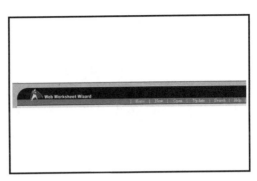

♦ This site allows teachers to create lessons, worksheets, or a class page on the Web quickly and without hassle (for students, see Project Poster). It allows instructors to create their own Web documents with images, hyperlinks, and e-mail links. Instructors may also search for existing worksheets by keyword, date, grade level, or subject.

Project Poster

http://poster.hprtec.org/

♦ This site allows students to post their projects on the Web. Students may place the page title, report title, text, an image, and links to other sites.

Assign-A-Day

http://assignaday.4teachers.org/

♦ Assign-A-Day is a free tool that allow students to communicate through an online teacher-managed calendar. Students can view assignments, schedules, or events for their classes.

Puzzlemaker

http://puzzlemaker.school.discovery.com/

♦ Puzzlemaker is a puzzle generation tool for teachers, students, and parents. Users can create and print customized word searches, crossword puzzles, and math puzzles using word lists.

Text Tool for Microsoft Word

http://www.teachers-pet.org

♦ Text Tool and Resource Search Tool are free installations that work in Microsoft Word. They allow teachers or students to create flashcards, gap-fill exercises, multiple-choice exercises, word and sentence jumbles, pronunciation and punctuation exercises, paragraph exercises, store word lists, and more.

GetFast

http://www.getfast.ca

- ◆ FAST (Free Assessment Summary Tool) is a tool for anonymous surveys that gives the teachers immediate results directly online. Send your students to the site to answer the questions, and with a click of your mouse, you have the results.

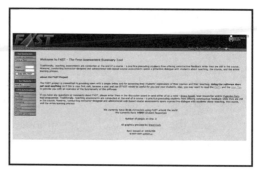

WebAuthor

http://ccat.sas.upenn.edu/plc/larrc/webauthor.html

- ◆ WebAuthor is tool for making online exercises.

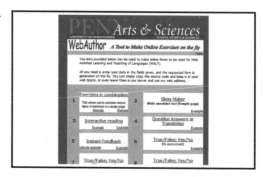

PowerPoint Games

http://www.gpschools.org/ci/ce/elem/elcom/summer/ppgames.htm

- ◆ This site offers downloadable Microsoft PowerPoint games and templates to create your own in the classroom.

QuizCenter

http://school.discovery.com/quizcenter/quizcenter.html

- ◆ QuizCenter is a Web-based tool that allows teachers to create, administer, and grade quizzes online. Quizzes are easy to develop and can be stored in a custom classroom. The site allows automatic correction, with results either displayed on the site or e-mailed to you. This application is password protected and offers an option for instructors to edit, delete, or create new quizzes.

E. L. Easton Exercises, Quizzes, Tests

http://eleaston.com/quizzes.html

- ◆ Choose from a variety of templates to create your own exercises, quizzes, and tests in Chinese, French, German, Italian, Japanese, Latin, Russian, and Spanish. The site also provides a list of applications from Hot Potatoes, WebCT, and Quiz Star that teachers can use to create their own exercise, quizzes, and tests.

Quia

http://www.quia.com/web

♦ Quia provides ready-made activities and quizzes in more than 50 subject areas, as well as templates for creating flashcards, word searches, ordered lists, jumbled words, hangman games, cloze exercises, patterns, scavenger hunts, and concentration games. It also has a tool for creating online quizzes, class Web pages, online surveys, and calendars and schedules. The Quia Directory encompasses a variety of free activities on English for French speakers, Advanced Placement Spanish literature, Chinese, Danish, Dutch, German, German geography, German literature, Dutch, Greek, Hawaiian, Hebrew, Hungarian, Indonesian, Irish, Italian, Japanese, Korean, Latin, Norwegian, Portuguese, Russian, Samoan, Spanish, simple Spanish grammar, Spanish for French speakers, Slovak, Swedish, and Turkish. Other functions require a subscription fee. A free 30-day trial is offered for those interested in purchasing.

Interactive Exercise Makers

http://lang.swarthmore.edu/makers/

♦ The Interactive Exercise Makers allow you to create exercises without any knowledge of computer programming languages. The exercises can be downloaded to your own computer or the school's Web server. Activities include GlossMaker (online text with annotations or glosses and media files or images), Cloze (fill-in exercises with sound files), MatchMaker (two-column matching exercises), MultiMaker (multiple-choice questions), MatchMaker 2 (DHTML for drag-and-drop images to text cues), PlaceMaker (true/false drag-and-drop exercises with vocabulary words), PlaceMaker 2 (true/false drag-and-drop exercise with two images and vocabulary words), PlaceMaker 3 (drag-and-drop exercises with vocabulary words that fit a specific location in an image), OrderMaker (drag-and-drop exercises with sentence parts), and MemoryMaker (memory and concentration exercises).

Software Resources

http://www.priorywoods.middlesbrough.sch.uk/resources/program/programres.htm

♦ Created by Priory Woods School in Middlesbrough, United Kingdom, this site offers a range of templates, add-ons, and activities. The templates can be adapted for many foreign languages.

RealProducer 10

http://www.realnetworks.com/products/producer/

♦ Formerly known as Helix Producer, this is a free downloadable tool to convert .wav files into RealAudio files. To download the free version, click on **Free RealProducer 10 Basic**.

DubIt

http://www.techsmith.com/products/dubit/default.asp

♦ DubIt allows you to create movie clips with voice narration, annotate images, create screen captures, send movies by e-mail, and narrate images or video clips.

Foreign Language Search Engines

http://facweb.furman.edu/%7Epecoy/mfl195/searchen.htm

♦ This site offer a list of search engines in English, French, German, and Spanish.

Fingertip Software

http://cyrillic.com/index.html

♦ This site offer fonts, software, and keyboards for multilingual computing.

Dr. Berlin's Foreign Font Archive

http://user.dtcc.edu/~berlin/fonts.html

♦ This is a resource site for foreign language characters, fonts, and keyboard utilities. The downloadable application is available as freeware, shareware, or public domain software and should be downloaded at your own risk.

SIL Encore IPA Fonts

http://scripts.sil.org/cms/scripts/page.php?site_id=

♦ This site, developed by SIL International: Partners in Language Development, offers IPA fonts of phonetic texts for both Mac and Windows systems. The IPA font download is free.

World Radio Locator

http://www.radio-locator.com/cgi-bin/nation

♦ Search for international radio stations in Africa, Asia, Australia and Oceania, Europe, the Middle East, North America, and South America.